IN CHRIST'S IMA

LEVEL I
TRACK ONE

CHRISTLIKENESS

TAKEN FROM WRITINGS BY

PASTOR FRANCIS FRANGIPANE

CHRISTLIKENESS

In Christ's Image Training
Web: www.ICITC.org

Published by
Arrow Publications Inc.
P.O. Box 10102
Cedar Rapids, IA 52410
Phone: 1-319-395-7833, 1-877-363-6889
Fax: 1-319-395-7353
Web: www.ArrowBookstore.com

CONTENTS

ONLINE, AT HOME
OR AT CHURCH

Originally, these lessons were compiled solely for our *In Christ's Image Training (ICIT)* online school. Both the content and sequencing of lessons were laboriously studied and prayed over; we desired, above all, to present foundational material that would literally endure into eternity itself.

ICIT students register online and then receive two written messages each week via email. They also receive a set of 39 audio teachings (on 24 CDs or MP3s), which complement the written messages and add to the training. Students are then tested every six weeks and receive a cumulative grade at the end of six months. In addition, they are given an opportunity to attend annual on-site training seminars with other passionate students from around the world, take advanced training, and eventually become part of an association that helps strengthen and inspire Christlikeness in support of their local churches or denominations.

Increasingly, however, people were asking if we would print the study manuals and make them available outside the structure of *ICIT.* Some who asked were pastors who wanted to integrate the training into their own church programs; others were individuals simply desiring the basic teachings for their own edification. After much prayer, we decided to allow these four manuals to be published and more widely distributed, which is why you have this manual in your hand. We realize, however, that this basic training may actually awaken a deeper desire for further resources. If so, you may want to participate in the advanced training offered by our school.

In order to qualify for admission to *In Christ's Image Training* school, you will need to purchase and study the audio messages. Then you will need to take a separate exam that will confirm to us that you have, indeed, understood the training materials and are, in fact, pursuing the character of Christ. For more information about testing and receiving a certificate of completion for Level I and then enrolling in the school via Level II, please see the *In Christ's Image Training* pages in the back of the manual.

Introduction

The Church and the Harvest

Today, perhaps more than at any other time in history, nations stand at a crossroads. In the midst of terror attacks, blatant rebellion and worldwide conflicts, is there yet one more "great awakening" in God's heart that will sweep multitudes into His kingdom? Or is the future irreversibly clocked, ever ticking toward catastrophic conflicts and doom? I, for one, am convinced that the Lord's heart burns for the nations. I believe that a great harvest season awaits us.

It is easy to see sin and predict doom. Yet, the very fact that God gives us the privilege of prayer tells us He desires we participate with Him in the transformation of our world. Indeed, even when a nation seems fully in the grip of evil, the heart of God is searching for one who would "stand in the gap before [Him] for the land." God's heart is to redeem, "not destroy" (Ezek. 22:30). What a tremendous insight into the nature of God, that if just one person embraces Christlike transformation – if he or she stands in the gap in unoffendable intercession – that individual can alter the future of a nation! Before you think I am exaggerating, both the Bible and secular history tell us this is exactly the case. Singular individuals have stood for their families, churches, cities and nations, and throughout time God has used them to alter the course of history (Heb. 11; Eccl. 9:15).

The key to unlocking this great power from God is to live life with one compelling goal: to obtain the likeness of Christ. Everything about our *ICIT* course is designed to focus our faith upon Jesus Christ. The priorities we present, if properly assimilated, will empower each of us to possess true spiritual transformation.

Our vision at *In Christ's Image Training* is to train and release hundreds of thousands of Christlike pastors, leaders and intercessors into countries throughout the world. We are entering the season of our greatest transformation; it is accelerating toward us. God wants to use us to reach our families, neighbors and beyond. But first He must renew and transform our hearts. Do not doubt that the Spirit of God can do a deep and thorough work in you. At the end of the age, the Lord has promised His work of raising up people and reaching the nations will be accomplished "thoroughly and quickly" (Rom. 9:28). Take faith! He assures us He will "hasten" our transformation "in its time" (Isa. 60:22).

A Word about These Lessons and Impartation

The Process of Divine Quickening

There are many components that must converge to produce healthy spiritual growth. We need faith in God, genuine humility and a living prayer life. We also need true grounding in God's Word and a doctrinal knowledge of our salvation as new covenant people. We must also posture our hearts in yielded dependence upon the Holy Spirit with the primary goal of attaining the likeness of Christ. Added to these (and other graces from God), there is yet one more gift the Holy Spirit supplies to accelerate our progress: impartation.

The fact is, principles of impartation are already working in us, but we may not be aware of them. Negatively speaking, it is the principle of impartation through which the "iniquity of the fathers" is transferred "on the children" (Exod. 20:5). The effect of negative impartation is seen each time "bad company corrupts good morals" (1 Cor. 15:33). It's also the reason why, when we listen to slander, our perception darkens each time we think about or talk to the slandered person. Something void of love was imparted to us from the critical person.

However, it is the positive aspects of godly impartation that we want to focus upon here. Indeed, Jesus was speaking of godly impartation when He taught, "He who receives a prophet in the name of a prophet shall receive a prophet's reward; and he who receives a righteous man in the name of a righteous man shall receive a righteous man's reward" (Matt. 10:41). Including the previous introductory verse (v. 40), Jesus mentions eight times in two sentences the words *receive* or *receives.* He is speaking not only of identification but of the larger flow of life from one to another via impartation. When we receive the Son, we are actually receiving the substance of the Father, also.

However, the flow of life is not contained within the Godhead. Jesus then says that His Spirit would actually accompany and flow through those whom He sends. People would see in Peter and John and the others the imparted power and authority of Jesus Himself. Finally, He adds that the principle of impartation would continue. Prophets and righteous men, if they were received correctly, could transfer their reward to others, so that the grace and power that God has worked in one, ultimately, could be transferred to many.

Now, when Jesus speaks of a prophet's (or righteous man's) reward, He is identifying a precious, living grace, a "holy consequence" to God's dealings in a leader's life. It is the reward of their sufferings, of going through hell to possess the substance of Heaven – and we can receive that reward simply by humbly recognizing God's work in another's life, receiving them, and receiving a measure of their gift through their ministry. Thus we obtain in a relatively short time what perhaps took them a lifetime to attain.

The Lord told Moses, "lay your hand" on Joshua and "put some of your authority on him" (Num. 27:15–23). *To ordain* in the Hebrew language meant, in part, "to fill the hands." Moses, as one whose own hands were filled with the spirit-overflow of his relationship with God, laid his hand upon his protege, Joshua, and Joshua walked in new authority. However, Joshua did not *attain* new authority, it was imparted to him.

Or consider Elijah, the prophet, as he trained Elisha, a farmer, to be his successor. At the end of a short, intense season of obedience, Elisha received a double portion of the spirit of Elijah (2 Kings 2). Elisha didn't just stay focused on the prophet, but he eagerly and legitimately sought the "prophet's reward." Both Joshua and Elisha received what God had worked in their predecessors. They became individuals who received from leaders and then, in many ways, did greater works than those who preceded them.

You see, submitting ourselves to receive from others does not diminish us; it expands us. We receive their reward without losing our uniqueness. Let's put a guard here, however. Elisha received a double portion of Elijah's spirit, but he never copied Elijah's personality or mannerisms. Be aware that if you find yourself mimicking a leader's mannerisms or style, you are probably focused on the wrong objective. It's the work of Christ in their spirit, not their personality, that we seek to appropriate.

When I speak of impartation, I do not only mean teaching. I also mean guided training, disciplining, and then releasing a man or woman of God into a ministry, all accomplished at the proper time with sufficient power. This is not to diminish the important aspect of teaching, but we need individuals who can both explain what the word *anointing* meant in the Bible and then, as the Lord leads, replicate their anointing in others.

God Gave Gifts to Men

What I am saying is that the goal of godly impartation is not only to inform but also to empower. Again, I do not want to minimize the value of those who serve as spiritual teachers. The fact is, many leaders are *already* imparting much through their teaching ministry; they just haven't defined it as such. If your pastor's influence in your life is noteworthy and transforming – if he or she *inspires* you – you are already receiving impartation and empowerment from God through that individual.

Yet some Christians in the Western world have withdrawn from the idea of impartation and drawing from other leaders. Even though the Bible mentions the "laying on of hands" in many places (Mark 16:18; 2 Tim. 1:6; Heb. 6:2, etc.) and it speaks openly about impartation (Rom. 1:11; 1 Thess. 2:8), they still consider the concept of impartation to be extra-biblical in nature. But clearly, God has intended to build up His church through His work in godly leaders. If this were not so, we would not have the Bible, for it was written by men whom God used.

However, let me put another guard here so there are no misunderstandings. The first place we must hear from the Lord is through the Scriptures (Matt. 22:29; 2 Tim. 3:16–17). Then we have the obligation to hear and obey what the Holy Spirit speaks to our hearts (Heb. 4:7, 12). God can also inspire us through nature and His creation (Ps. 19:1; Rom. 1:20). All these are gifts through which the Spirit of God can build us up and communicate to our hearts.

There is another means of training: the Bible tells us that "when [Christ] ascended on high … He gave gifts to men" (Eph. 4:8). While Christ certainly gave us many gifts, the *specific* gifts mentioned in the context of Paul's discourse are transformed men. "He gave some as apostles, and some as prophets, and some as evangelists, and some as pastors and teachers" (Eph. 4:11). Bible scholars refer to these individuals as "gift ministries," for each of them, to the degree they genuinely are conformed to aspects of the nature of Christ, are gifts from the Lord to His people. Their divinely appointed task is the "equipping of the saints for the work of service, to the building up of the body of Christ" (v. 12). Their task, in brief, is to train and impart.

Let's bring the context of these verses into the twenty-first century. Let's also recognize with joy and humility that it is a good thing to receive impartation from godly fathers and mothers, individuals who are walking in some measure of mature Christlikeness. Remember, we are not submitting to them blindly. The leaders whom God uses in our lives are not "blind guides of the blind," as the Pharisees were (Matt. 15:14); they are leaders with vision helping others with vision to see clearer. We are simply recognizing those who have victory in an area in which we are weak, and receiving through them a means to achieve our own victory in Christ through their help.

How to Receive Impartation

The American Heritage dictionary defines *to impart* as "to grant a share of; bestow; to make known, disclose; to pass on, transmit." Paul wrote the church in Rome that he desired to "impart some spiritual gift ... that you may be established" (Rom. 1:11). Paul told the Thessalonian Christians that he and his team were "well-pleased to impart ... not only the gospel of God but also our own lives" (1 Thess. 2:8). The word *impart* in the Greek text means just as it does in English: "to give over, to share, to impart."

There are many ways we can receive from others. In fact, two of the men who most influenced my spiritual life were Watchman Nee and Andrew Murray, both of whom had been dead many years when I discovered their books. In 1970 I found

Watchman Nee's book, *The Release of the Spirit;* it was the first Christian book I read. A couple years later I came across Andrew Murray's works. In a real way, he became a mentor to me. I would kneel at the foot of my bed with his material and pray, underlining and taking notes. *Like Christ* and *Waiting on God* were powerful influences in defining my spirituality, and I would return to Murray's books over and over again. His passion for Jesus fueled my passion. God used these men, and many others, to build into the foundational structure of my heart.

Most importantly, of course, even when we submit to men, our quest is to possess the heart of Christ as it lives in them. It is Christ we seek to know, not merely those He sends. Thus, even as we appreciate those whom God sends, our passion is to develop an abiding relationship with Christ Himself, that every area of our life might be filled up with Him.

What makes our relationship with the Lord Jesus *functional* is the reality of His *imparted* life and transferred righteousness. Jesus taught, "I am the vine, you are the branches; he who abides in Me, and I in him, he bears much fruit, for apart from Me you can do nothing" (John 15:5). The life that flows directly from Christ, "the vine," into us, His "branches," speaks of receiving from Him through the power of divine impartation. He's called us to abide in Him, and for His words to abide in us (John 15:7). Thus, as I pray, as I worship and seek Him, I also take God's Word to the foot of my bed and kneel and study, often placing several translations side by side in my pursuit of knowing Him.

During one period of my life, for over three years, all I read each day were the gospels and excerpts from more than a hundred commentaries that gave insights into what Jesus taught. To this day, in spite of how busy my life becomes, I seek to read the Bible through each year, maintaining my passion to know Christ, my Redeemer King.

Remember, although impartation brings about accelerated spiritual growth, we are not looking to compromise, or seeking shortcuts. We simply want to take full advantage of the variety of ways through which God can transform us. Allow your hunger to be an indicator of where you should go for training. Are you hungry to function more effectively in prayer or spiritual gifts, deliverance or evangelism? Perhaps you desire to deepen your worship of God or your intimacy with Him. The Bible tells us to "work out your salvation with fear and trembling; for it is God who is at work in you, both to will and to work for His good pleasure" (Phil. 2:12–13). We "work out" what God is "working in."

You see, inner hunger is a work from God (Matt. 5:6), an indicator of His direction for your life. Let your hunger guide you to someone who is clearly ahead of you along the way. See if they have materials or a school where you can train, either by correspondence or in actual attendance. At the very least, when you find someone whose ministry stirs your heart, get their materials, kneel at the foot of your bed, and ask God to make every morsel of truth a part of your life.

At *In Christ's Image Training* our quest is to intensify your focus upon attaining Christlikeness. Our vision is to see hundreds of thousands of Christlike pastors, leaders and intercessors standing before God on behalf of the world around them. When you conclude your studies with us, there are many others who will impart values and giftings into your life. Hopefully, what you've learned with us will have increased your ability to receive from others. Together, let us all seek to build upon the eternal foundation, which is Christ Himself (1 Cor. 3:9–11).

Our successful *ICIT* students will receive a living impartation from the materials available. You will possess more than the correct answers to theological questions. After studying this first manual, you will know you've passed this course if your highest passion is to attain Christlikeness. I will tell you in advance the "correct answers" for the next three manuals: your heart trembles in humility when God speaks; you intercede for others instead of just finding fault; and you are a peacemaker who works to build Christ-centered unity in your family, church and city. Our successful students will be noticeably marked by this one thing: they will be unoffendable while in pursuit of their vision, even if they suffer persecution, spiritual warfare or terrible injustices along the way.

I also expect that when fearsome times come – and we will indeed face such times – our students will be among the most courageous. They will stand when others might faint or flee. Other ministries might be graced so people "fall under the power." Our goal is to empower you to stand. Yes, even in times when "darkness will cover the earth, and deep darkness the peoples," the successful *ICIT* student will remain steadfast, trusting in God's goodness, expecting that "the Lord will rise upon [them] and His glory will appear upon [them]." Among our numbers will be those who persevere until "nations … come to [their] light, and kings to the brightness of [their] rising" (Isa. 60:2–3).

Session One:

The Vision:

Becoming Christlike

But we all, with unveiled face, beholding as in a mirror the glory of the Lord, are being transformed into the same image from glory to glory, just as from the Lord, the Spirit.   *—2 Corinthians 3:18*

SESSION ONE AUDIO MESSAGES:

1a. Personal Welcome from Francis
1b. Our Goal Is Christ

Lessons are to be distributed from
the Training Center only, please.

CHAPTER ONE

ONE PURPOSE: REVEAL THE FULLNESS OF CHRIST

The virtue of any institution is not so much in its doctrines or organization; rather, its virtue resides in the quality of person it produces.

A NEW AND FRESH ANOINTING

Some of you have been struggling, not knowing what God has for you. You have been through a season in which the Lord has revealed your need of Him in very dramatic ways. Jesus Himself has been near to you; however, His closeness was not merely in the way of external blessings but in the way of His cross. Yet you have delighted in this, for the way of the cross has increasingly become the way of your life.

At the same time, many of your ideas and programs that once seemed compelling now seem weak and ineffectual. Even some of your favorite Christian themes, as well as church government in general, have been reduced to a simpler, purer definition of Christianity. You just want to know

Jesus. Because this breaking has been God working in you, you are uplifted.

In the midst of the changes you have been through, one conviction has grown ever brighter: your goal is to see the character of Jesus Christ, His meekness, authority and love manifested in your life. You have discovered that any other program or church activity that does not reveal Jesus is a "dead work"; although well-intentioned, they are powerless to effectively transform the people.

The truth is, the Holy Spirit is preparing you for a new and fresh anointing from the Lord. Ultimately, God will use you to inspire holiness in the church and to shatter the demonic strongholds corrupting your city.

POSSESSING THE FULLNESS OF CHRIST

We have instructed the church in nearly everything but becoming disciples of Jesus Christ. We have filled the people with doctrines instead of Deity; we have given them manuals instead of Emmanuel. It is not difficult to recognize someone from Pentecostal, Baptist, charismatic or other traditional church backgrounds. Nearly every congregation seems to develop a particular slant or system of traditions, some of which ultimately obscures the simplicity and purity of devotion to Christ. We can honor our traditions, but we must not be limited by them. For us, they will never be enough. We are seeking to be like Jesus, not men. We want the kingdom of God, not typical American Christianity.

Thus, as a man of God, I must be vigilant to submit myself, above all things, to the Spirit and words of the Lord Jesus, incessantly reaching for the holy standards of the kingdom of God. I consider that any focus or goal other than Christ Himself *in fullness* will become a source of deception in the days ahead.

Look at what Jesus did with common people. In just three and a half years, average men and women were transformed into fearless disciples, literally filled with the Spirit of God! They did not wince at suffering; they did not withdraw from sacrifice. These once ordinary people were equipped with spiritual authority over demons and exercised power over illnesses. They were the living proof that Christ transforms people.

Three and a half years of undiluted Jesus will produce in us what it did in them: the kingdom of God!

The first disciples were as average and human as we are. The difference between them and us is Jesus. He is the only difference.

One may argue that this occurred two thousand years ago. True, but "Jesus Christ is the same yesterday and today, yes and forever" (Heb. 13:8). You may say, "But they actually heard Jesus speak; they saw His miracles!" The same Spirit that worked through Jesus in the first century is poured out upon us today. The Holy Spirit has not grown old and feeble; He is still poured out today. The words Jesus uttered in the first century are still "living and active" today (Heb. 4:12), even to the "end of the age" (Matt. 28:20). You see, we have no excuses.

The eternal One who established His kingdom in men two millennia ago is fully capable of producing it in us today. All we need is undiluted, uninhibited Jesus. All we need are hearts that will not be satisfied with something or someone other than Him.

Let me make it plain: God is not raising up "ministries"; He is raising up bondslaves. After we recognize that the goal is not ministry but joyful slavery, we will begin to see the power of Christ restored to the church.

Thus the pattern for leadership in the years ahead is simple: leaders must be individuals whose burning passion is conformity to Jesus Christ. Therefore, pray for your leaders; pray with grace.

Is this not the highest passion of your heart, to possess the likeness of Christ? From Heaven's view, the issue with our congregations is not merely one procedure over another; the concern is, will we become people who are seeking hard after Christ?

DON'T ARGUE ABOUT CHURCH GOVERNMENT

God can use practically any church structure if the people in that congregation are genuinely seeking Him. On the day before Pentecost the Lord had a small church of one hundred twenty people in an upper room, but they had been earnestly seeking God. In Antioch there were prophets and teachers who were together in one heart seeking God (Acts 13:1). Through the last two millennia, the Lord had people who were passionate about seeking God, and God used the common men and women to bring revival and awakening.

The outward form is not the issue with the Almighty; the true issue is the posture of the human heart before Him. Do we want Christianity or Christlikeness? Are we passionate about possessing the fullness of Christ?

OBJECTIVE DESPERATION

We may argue church government and procedures, but the truth is that a move of God starts more "formless and void" than structured and well-organized. Hungry God-seeking individuals meeting in a basement or an upper room are the ones whom God uses. The Spirit graces them with *emptiness;* He pours into their hearts *objective desperation.* Relentlessly and purposefully they come before God, laying aside their attainments and skills. As Christ emptied Himself, so they also lay aside privileges and comforts and follow the pattern of Christ, taking His form, "the form of a bond-servant" (Phil. 2:7).

They bring their great barrenness to God, knowing that true fullness is always preceded by true emptiness. They view the knowledge of their spiritual poverty as a gift from God, a preparation for His kingdom (Matt. 5:3; Rev. 3:17). Is it not true that the greater the sense of emptiness within us, the stronger is our hunger for God?

Those whom God chooses are "new wineskins," cleansed, emptied and capable of expanding with the new wine. Their hearts are containers into which the Spirit of God is poured; they swell with Christ's inner fullness. The purpose of their lives is to contain the fruit and power of the Holy Spirit.

Our approach to God should not be rigidly structured and inflexible, but formless and soft. Let us become a people whose heart's passion is to seek God until Christ Himself is actually formed within us (Gal. 4:19).

Therefore, let us not make church government an issue. The priority is this: will we lay aside our ideas, return to the Gospels and obey what Jesus commands? Will we become objectively desperate in our search and hunger for God?

FIND JESUS, NOT JUST A RELIGION

In this new stirring of God, our goal as church leaders, intercessors, and members of the body of Christ is to abide in Jesus, not to elevate one denomination above another. John taught, "The one who says he abides in Him ought himself to walk in the same manner as He walked" (1 John 2:6). If we truly abide in Him, we will "walk even as He walked." Are there not a number of areas within each of us where Jesus has become more of a religion than a person?

The first-century saints had the words of Jesus, and they had the Spirit of Jesus. In that simplicity, the church enjoyed unsurpassed greatness and power. We also are returning to being His disciples, seeking to walk even as Jesus walked. This is the singular requirement in building the house of the Lord where the many are one: we must want Christ's image established in our hearts.

Is this possible? Are we being reasonable? Listen to what Jesus taught. He said, "He who believes in Me, the works that I do, he will do also; and greater works than these he will do; because I go to the Father" (John 14:12). He taught, "If you abide in Me, and My words abide in you, ask whatever you wish, and it will be done for you" (John 15:7). When we are aligned correctly to God's will, we will indeed have the Father's endorsement and the Son's authority.

Therefore, the Father's goal, which must become our goal, is nothing less than Christlikeness, where we become fully trained in the knowledge of the ways of God. The Lord calls us to pay the same price, do the same works, and possess the exact same benefits from prayer that Jesus did. We cannot afford to compromise what God has promised or disobey what He requires. These verses confirm that when the words of Jesus are taught, and where the Spirit of Jesus has liberty, the life of Jesus is manifested. Let this become both our immediate and our long-term goal: to see Jesus Christ revealed in His fullness in the church.

Let's pray: *Lord Jesus, forgive us for putting doctrines about church government and administration ahead of our love for You. Cleanse us, Master, of the effects of false religious traditions. Even at this moment, grant us unrestrained passion for You and You alone! For Your glory we live and pray. Amen.*

—FROM THE BOOK, *WHEN THE MANY ARE ONE*

SELF TEST, CHAPTER ONE

Remember, we are looking for answers that correspond with this train-ing. Please write out your answers, allowing the Holy Spirit to provoke your thoughts. You may want to use them for group discussion. Note: we do not provide answers to questions you write out. To check your multiple choice answers, see answer key in the next session.

Chapter 1, Question #1: In two paragraphs, what is the true value of any school or training organization?

Chapter 1, Question #2: What is the ultimate goal of the church?

1. An institution's virtue resides in:
   a. its flawless materials
   b. the quality of person it produces
   c. its financial condition
   d. its programs

2. As we grow in Christ we become more focused on one thing:
   a. to know the Old Testament
   b. authority
   c. creative ideas
   d. to know the heart of Jesus Christ

3. Any focus will become a source of deception in the days ahead unless it is:
   a. a mega church
   b. Christ Himself in fullness
   c. the worship service
   d. more programs

4. The only difference between the first disciples of Christ and ourselves is:
   a. email
   b. culture
   c. language classes
   d. they had 3½ years of undiluted Jesus

5. The eternal One is capable of producing in us all we need:
   a. sound government
   b. undiluted, uninhibited Jesus
   c. strong deacons
   d. singing

6. God is not raising up "ministries" but:
   a. church steeples
   b. church organists
   c. bondslaves
   d. Christian authors

7. The Lord used common men and women in every revival, but first they were each:
   a. credentialed by their denomination
   b. passionately seeking God
   c. seminary graduates
   d. good at taking offerings

8. We must be emptied as Christ emptied Himself because God chooses new wineskins that are:
   a. capable of expanding
   b. emptied
   c. cleansed
   d. all the above

Chapter Two

Consecrated For Christlikeness

"Without faith," the writer of Hebrews tells us, "it is impossible to please God" (Heb. 11:6). Faith is the substance of the things we are hoping for, the evidence of things not yet seen (Heb. 11:1). Hebrews continues explaining that by faith we understand that the visible has its origin in the invisible (v. 3 NEB). In other words, a person with faith has living within their spirit the substance of a reality that, though invisible to others, will inevitably manifest in time.

If we continue our study of Hebrews, we see a registry of people who had true, God-inspired faith. Today, to have faith means I believe Jesus died for my sins and that, because of Christ, I am going to Heaven. Certainly, this is where faith begins. However, Jesus is the author and *perfecter* of our faith. The faith Christ inspires not only gets us to Heaven when we die, but is capable of bringing Heaven to where we live. Thus, it is vital to note that everyone listed in Hebrew's "Hall of Faith" not only believed in God but was anointed to establish a God-reality into life's scheme that dramatically altered the course of the world.

Consider this summary thought from Hebrews, chapter 11:

And what more shall I say? For time will fail me if I tell of Gideon, Barak, Samson, Jephthah, of David and Samuel and the prophets, who by faith conquered kingdoms, performed acts of righteousness, obtained promises, shut the mouths of lions, quenched the power of fire, escaped the edge of the sword, from weakness were made strong, became mighty in war, put foreign armies to flight.

—Hebrews 11:32–34

People with faith were not just "believers"; they were world changers!

ALL THINGS ARE POSSIBLE

Today, many look at the iniquity in their nation and assume a certain doom perspective based on God's wrath upon sin. What they have not considered is the power and weight of the believing, praying church in the land. Jesus said that His people held the faith-future in their hands. He taught that whatever His disciples would "bind" would be enforced by Heaven; whatever His earthly followers "loosed" would be released by Heaven (Matt. 18:18).

Jesus did not say all things were possible for those who analyze, but for those who believe. Paul said that love believes all things (1 Cor. 13:7). When Jesus asks, "When the Son of Man comes, will He find faith in the earth?" (Luke 18:8), He is not doubting there will be faith, He is asking us as individuals: *Will I find faith in you?* We must choose to answer that question in the affirmative. Yes, I believe in You, Lord, and I believe You are the rewarder of those who diligently seek You (Heb. 11:6).

There is a deception that enters the mind once one accepts the idea that the only destiny for their nation is divine wrath. For once we accept such fatalistic thinking, we automatically exempt ourselves from having to pray or fast or love or sacrifice or stand in faith for national healing and revival. All that spiritually remains within us is an embittered, self-righteous soul that is angry with everyone who still has faith.

Remember, we are not saying that America is without sin. In some ways, the sin in our nation is more glaring, more defiant since September 11, 2001. Yet God's primary goal is not to destroy sinners, but that His people become Christlike. The charged, evil atmosphere in America (or whatever nation you are from) is a perfect environment to create Christlikeness in the church: our nations are in great need of prayer, love and faith, the very attributes that will perfect Christlikeness in us.

Thus, it is my conviction that America is not doomed to destruction, but destined for a spiritual awakening. How can I say that? Isaiah 52:15 tells us that Christ will "sprinkle many nations" and that "kings will shut their mouths on account of Him." Isaiah predicts a time when, by divine revelation, world leaders will "see and … understand."

Simply, I believe the power of the blood shed by Christ is greater than the power of sin in America.

The True Focus

Some believe the church will be raptured at any minute, while others are convinced that the church is about to enter some or all of the Tribulation. It is my conviction, however, that the next event in the unfolding of God's work is neither the Rapture nor Tribulation, but the establishing of Christlikeness in the church. This issue of Christlikeness in the church is the crown event, the pinnacle of all the redemptive works of God. It is the root cause of creation itself (Gen. 1:26).

Some say that the spiritual restoration of Israel is the Lord's focus; others revel in the gathering of the nations. But, in solemn truth, I say that there is nothing more important nor pivotal to the timing of last days events than the Christlikeness transformation that is now just beginning. My earnest, unceasing prayer is that this truth – Christ manifest in fullness through the church – would become the all consuming passion to everyone who calls upon God's name.

We have lived within a stronghold of unbelief concerning the spiritual character of the church. I call it the doctrine of continual sinfulness, as though we will never obtain spiritual maturity. No! There is a bride who shall find grace given to her to make herself ready, to put on fine linen, bright and clean! There is a church growing from glory to glory, being transformed into Christ's image! There are people who are overcomers, who shall inherit the promises of God!

We have learned to live with this staggering amount of compromise when, in fact, God is seeking to bring conformity to Christ.

If we do not have this vision of Christlikeness, our efforts will be no better than the Taliban's attempt to control the flesh. I don't want merely to control my flesh, but that in my life God's Word becomes flesh, my flesh!

> And He gave some as apostles, and some as prophets, and some as evangelists, and some as pastors and teachers, for the equipping of the saints for the work of service, to the building up of the body of Christ; until we all attain to the unity of the faith, and of the knowledge of the Son of God, to a mature man, to the measure of the stature which belongs to the fullness of Christ.
> —Ephesians 4:11–13

We are called to attain "the measure of the stature which belongs to the fullness of Christ." Do you see Christ's love? His love is the attainable standard for our love. Are you impressed with His faith? His faith is the measure we should see in our lives.

"For those whom He foreknew, He also pre-destined to become conformed to the image of His Son, so that He would be the firstborn among many brethren" (Rom. 8:29). If you don't have this vision, you cannot defeat the flesh; you can only hide it until you are out of church and no one is looking.

"The one who says he abides in Him ought himself to walk in the same manner as He walked" (1 John 2:6). Jesus said, "The works that I do, he will do also; and greater works than these he will do; because I go to the Father" (John 14:12). "Everyone who has this hope fixed on Him purifies himself, just as He is pure" (1 John 3:3). It is the hope of Christlikeness that produces the desire to purify ourselves, "just as He is pure."

What does this mean in terms of the world? God will release an army of Christlike saints. They will pray, not merely judge, when they see life's wrongs; they will offer themselves in intercession for the things that are evil. They will go extra miles and turn the other cheek. They will perfectly reveal the mercy of God, before the wrath of God is revealed.

Paul says, "We are ready to punish all disobedience, whenever your obedience is complete" (2 Cor. 10:6). He is talking about taking every thought captive to the obedience of Christ. What is the obedience of Christ? It is a soul fully given to the cause of redemption and mercy.

Let's pray: *Dear Jesus, You haven't called me to simply attend church, but to become a world changer. Master, forgive me for looking at the world with unbelief, as though You were incapable of using me to touch the lives of others. Lord, You are using this world to perfect my faith and purify my love. Speak this truth to me, O Righteous King, with revelation power. Amen!*

—FROM PASTOR FRANGIPANE'S EMAIL TEACHING

SELF TEST, CHAPTER TWO

Remember, we are looking for answers that correspond with this train-
ing. Please write out your answers, allowing the Holy Spirit to provoke
your thoughts. You may want to use them for group discussion. Note:
we do not provide answers to questions you write out. To check your
multiple choice answers, see answer key in the next session.

Chapter 2, Question #1: Explain in your own words the difference between having accurate theological knowledge and having faith. How are they connected? How are they distinct?

Chapter 2, Question #2: What areas in your world has God given you faith to see changed?

1. To the people in Hebrew's "Hall of Faith," faith meant:
    a. I don't forget to tithe
    b. through God, I can change the world
    c. properly organized doctrinal positions
    d. instant results

2. Jesus said all things are possible for those who:
    a. analyze
    b. study
    c. doubt
    d. believe

3. The Lord is the rewarder of those who:
    a. are avid readers
    b. diligently seek Him (Heb. 11:6)
    c. wear formal clothes at church
    d. watch Christian TV

4. The very attributes that will perfect Christlikeness in us are exactly what our nations need. They are:
    a. love
    b. prayer
    c. faith
    d. all the above

5. Pastor Francis calls it the "doctrine of continual sinfulness" when we:
    a. abide in grace
    b. live as though we will never obtain spiritual maturity
    c. seek grace
    d. become Christlike

6. Christ's love is the _____ standard for our love:
   a. unobtainable
   b. brotherly
   c. questionable
   d. attainable

7. We cannot defeat the flesh unless we have the vision to:
   a. become numero uno
   b. be conformed to the image of Christ
   c. see the handwriting on the wall
   d. tell it to behave

8. Obtaining the obedience of Christ so that mercy will triumph means:
   a. choosing our own sacrifices
   b. obeying the Ten Commandments
   c. going to church
   d. we strive for the perfection of love in all circumstances

QUOTE:

"When Jesus asks, 'When the Son of Man comes, will He find faith in the earth?' (Luke 18:8), He is not doubting there will be faith, He is asking us as individuals: 'Will I find faith in you?' "

Track One: Christlikeness

Session Two:

The Preeminence of Christ's Words

"He who rejects Me and does not receive My sayings, has one who judges him; the word I spoke is what will judge him at the last day."

—*John 12:48*

SESSION TWO AUDIO MESSAGES:

2a. God's Power in a Holy Life
2b. More of God

Lessons are to be distributed from
the Training Center only, please.

ANSWER KEY TO LAST SESSION'S
SELF TEST QUESTIONS:

CHAPTER ONE. One Purpose: Reveal the
Fullness of Christ
1.b, 2.d, 3.b, 4.d, 5.b, 6.c, 7.b, 8.d.

CHAPTER TWO. Consecrated for Christlikeness
1.b, 2.d, 3.b, 4.d, 5.b, 6.d, 7.b, 8.d.

CHAPTER THREE

KEEPING YOUR WAY PURE

The Scriptures tell us that the Lord is our keeper. To be kept by Him, however, does not mean we will not face temptations, for even Jesus was tempted. Rather, it is in the midst of trials and temptations that God keeps us. And the way He keeps us is through His Word. Therefore, if we would be holy, we must know intimately the person whom the Bible calls the Word.

TREASURING THE WORD

How can a young man keep his way pure? By keeping it according to Your word. With all my heart I have sought You; do not let me wander from Your commandments. Your word I have treasured in my heart, that I may not sin against You.

—Psalm 119:9–11

The question is not, "How can a young man become pure?" as though purity of heart was impossible for a young man. Rather, the question is, "How can he *keep* his way pure?" Purity of heart can be reached and maintained if we abide in fellowship with God's Word.

No matter what our age may be, we keep our way pure by "keeping it according to [God's] word … [which] I have treasured in my heart" (Ps. 119:9, 11). There is a place beyond knowing a few Bible verses, a place where the living Word of God becomes our most treasured possession. To treasure the Word is to love it, even as it pierces "as far as the division of soul and spirit" (Heb. 4:12).

To treasure the Word is to remain fully vulnerable, even as it judges "the thoughts and intentions of the heart" (Heb. 4:12). It exposes our motives. It is the lamp of the Spirit, which illuminates the darkness of our hearts with light. It sets us free from the strongholds of hidden sin. It wounds, but it also heals, penetrating deeply into the very core of our being. The Word of the Lord, united with the Holy Spirit, is the vehicle of our transformation into the image of Christ. Holiness comes to him whose treasure is the Word.

The Word Is God

Many read the Scriptures simply to reinforce their current beliefs. Although they read the entire Bible, their mind only sees certain doctrines. Instead of believing what they read, they merely read what they already believe. Rarely do they find new truths in the Word. Baptists see from their perspective, Pentecostals and charismatics each have theirs, while Catholics and other denominations often have a completely different emphasis. The same way the Jews were "baptized into Moses" (1 Cor. 10:2), so Christians are often baptized into their denomination. When they are fully indoctrinated, their minds have been immersed into a pool of teaching that leaves them more conformed to the image of their sect than to the likeness of Christ.

But if we would grow in Christ's likeness, we must be baptized into Christ's Spirit, not the spirit or slant of any particular denomination. When one is baptized in Christ, his spirit is actually clothed with Christ (Gal. 3:27). It is Christ's image in holiness and power that a true disciple seeks. We cannot allow ourselves to be inoculated with a dozen or so special Bible verses that merely get us "saved" but leave us immune from the fullness of God! You are a disciple of Jesus Christ: the reality of God's kingdom is found in the combined meaning of all Jesus taught. Therefore, you must treasure every word!

The Word is God. The Scriptures are not God, but *the Spirit that breathes through the words is God.* And this Holy Spirit should be honored as God. Therefore, as you seek the Lord, place your Bible at the foot of your bed, and kneel as you read; are you not seeking to meet with the Almighty? Pray that you will not merely read intellectually. Rather, ask the Holy Spirit to speak to your heart through the Word.

To be a true disciple, you must tremble when God speaks (Isa. 66:2). Prepare your heart with reverence and worship. As you kneel in humility before the Lord, the Word will be engrafted into your soul, actually becoming a part of your nature (James 1:21).

Again, do not read only to reinforce your established doctrines, although prayerful consideration of another's understanding may be of value. Be prepared to take notes, to write down what the Spirit says, being ever mindful that it is the quickening Spirit, not the letter, that brings life (2 Cor. 3:6).

Read with an attitude of willingness, humility and repentance, and even if you cannot fully obey the Word, keep it, holding it in your heart. Right here is where most people fall short. For if the command seems impossible or unreasonable to their minds, they disregard it. But Jesus said, "He who has My commandments and keeps them is the one who loves Me" (John 14:21). Many times, *before you are able to obey the Word, you must make yourself keep it.* God must work in you "both to will and to work" (Phil. 2:13). First God makes you willing, and then He makes you able.

In this process, let the Word pierce you; let it crucify you. Suffer with it, but do not let it go. View every Bible command, every "Thou shall be" as a promise God will fulfill in your life as you steadfastly keep His Word. And as you keep the Word, treasuring His commandment in your heart, the Word itself will effectually work within you, bringing grace and transformation as you believe.

Each of us needs to stockpile in our minds as much of the Bible as we can. During the first ten years of my walk with God, I began my daily study by reading five chapters in the Pentateuch (the first five books of the Bible). I would then read aloud five psalms, seeking to express in my reading the emotion and faith of the psalmist. I would carefully study one chapter of Proverbs and three chapters in the Prophets. Then I would read three chapters in one of the New Testament Epistles and finally one chapter in the Gospels. In all, I studied about eighteen chapters a day. Reading in this way kept me balanced in the various truths of the Bible.

Perhaps you cannot do as much, but just four chapters a day will complete the whole Bible in less than a year. Whatever approach you decide upon, combine Old and New Testaments in your pursuit. I would keep my pattern diligently until the Holy Spirit began to speak or "breathe" through the Scriptures. When the Spirit spoke, I honored Him by following His leading, being careful to write down all that He taught. The next day I would begin my pattern again by kneeling before the Word, picking up my study where I left off.

Carry a pad and pen with you at all times. At night, put your notebook at your bedside, for God will speak to His beloved, even in his sleep. We are called to *abide* in Him, not just visit with Him.

Ultimately, we must be fully given to the words of Jesus. The Gospels must rise to preeminence above all other books in the Bible. Too often Christians preach Paul or another one of the apostles more than Jesus. Yet Paul taught, "Let the word of Christ richly dwell within you" (Col. 3:16). It was the word of Christ that transformed all the apostles. The apostle John taught, "Anyone who goes too far and does not abide in the teaching of Christ, does not have God" (2 John 1:9).

We are called to abide in the teaching of Christ! Yet, typically, Christians have spent little time in Christ's words, choosing rather to read about Him than dwell within Him. We have "how-to" books for every facet of existence. We have come to believe that *reading books* is the essence of Christianity! We are ever learning but never coming to the knowledge of the truth (2 Tim. 3:7). Dear ones, *truth is in Jesus* (Eph. 4:21).

Therefore, we must learn to abide in the teachings of Christ, even while we pursue our study of the rest of the Scriptures. Only Jesus died for our sins; our pursuit of *Him* must become the singular goal of our spiritual endeavors.

You must develop such a listening ear that the Spirit could speak to you anywhere about anything. Honor Him and He will honor you. Keep the Word in your heart, and He will establish you in holiness before God. He will keep your way pure.

Let's pray: *Lord Jesus, thank You for working in me, for making me both willing and increasingly able to do Your will. I love Your Word, O God. As I keep it, may it also keep me and make my way pure. Amen.*

—FROM THE BOOK
HOLINESS, TRUTH AND THE PRESENCE OF GOD

SELF TEST, CHAPTER THREE

Remember, we are looking for answers that correspond with this training. Please write out your answers, allowing the Holy Spirit to provoke your thoughts. You may want to use them for group discussion. Note: we do not provide answers to questions you write out. To check your multiple choice answers, see answer key in the next session.

Chapter 3, Question #1: What does it mean to be a disciple of Jesus Christ?

Chapter 3, Question #2: In what ways does the Word of God shape your approach to life?

I. If we would be holy, we must:
   a. read the Law out loud
   b. memorize the church bylaws
   c. promise our pastor never to sin again
   d. know the Word of God

2. Holiness comes to him whose treasure is:
   a. deep within
   b. the Word
   c. silver and gold
   d. hidden in the field

3. To grow in Christ's likeness, we must be:
   a. reinforcing our current beliefs
   b. immersed in doctrine
   c. baptized in His Spirit
   d. baptized into our denomination

4. It is the _____ that brings life (2 Cor. 3:6)
   a. letter of the Law
   b. quickening Spirit
   c. memorization
   d. pastor

5. God must work in you both to _____.
   a. bind and to loose
   b. build up and to tear down
   c. will and to work
   d. see and to hear

6. When the Spirit speaks:
   a. everybody listens
   b. write it down
   c. wait until you feel goose bumps, then shout
   d. it will always be about sin in your life

7. We must develop such a listening ear that the Spirit can speak to us:
   a. in the tongues of angels
   b. anywhere
   c. about anything
   d. both b & c

QUOTE:

"You are a disciple of Jesus Christ: the reality of God's kingdom is found in the combined meaning of all Jesus taught. Therefore, you must treasure every word!"

CHAPTER FOUR

DEVOTED TO JESUS' WORDS

Many people want to be saved *from* God. They don't really want intimacy with the words of God, where His Spirit penetrates their hearts and changes them. They want something that inoculates them with just enough religion on Sunday to immunize them from God the rest of the week.

Many of us have been taught that Jesus' words are either for the Jews or the Millennium or the first century. I cannot help but condemn such doctrine as deception. How can we say we love Him and not do as He says? Jesus said, "If you love Me, you will keep My commandments" (John 14:15). If you love Jesus, you *want* to keep His commandments.

People who do not know Jesus' heart read His words and consider them too hard. Their problem lies in the fact that they have missed His grace. Both grace and truth are realized in Jesus. When Jesus gives you something that seems impossible, He provides the grace to accomplish it. At times, you may feel unable to obey His commands immediately. Keep them in your heart, however, and hold them fast. Know that His words are for you, for today, and desire them fervently. Gladly bear any necessary discomfort in this process. Welcome

Jesus' words with meekness, for once they are planted within us they are grafted into our natures and are able to save our souls.

"If you abide in Me, and My words abide in you, ask whatever you wish, and it shall be done for you" (John 15:7). Can you see why Satan wants to keep you from Jesus' words? Abiding in Him puts *power* in your prayer life!

You will never have a greater meeting with God than when He comes living and breathing through the Scriptures into your heart. At that moment the very same Spirit that hovered over creation in the beginning is hovering over you, transforming you into the image of Christ through the Word. That living, breathing Word is God!

On the Mount of Transfiguration, in the midst of the glory of God, Peter sought to go and build "three tabernacles" (Matt. 17:4). He wanted to come up with a program to organize what God was doing. A cloud covered the mountain and the voice of the Father spoke, *"This is My beloved Son, with whom I am well-pleased; listen to Him!"* (Matt. 17:5, *italics mine*). This is the intense desire in the heart of the Father, that we would forsake our various programs and gimmicks and, instead, simply listen to Jesus! Do not laugh at Peter's action, for the same glory is just as close to us as it was to him – as is the same instinct to revert to dead works in spite of who we have seen.

MY WORD WILL JUDGE YOU

"If anyone hears My sayings and does not keep them, I do not judge him; for I did not come to judge the world, but to save the world. He who rejects Me and does not receive My sayings, has one who judges him; the word I spoke is what will judge him at the last day."   —John 12:47–48

Jesus came to save the world. He states clearly that He did not come to judge it. Both the way He saves us and the way He judges us is through His Word. If we do His Word, it will save us. If we reject His Word, it will judge us. It is the Word He speaks and our response to His Word that determines salvation or condemnation. If we have called Him, "Lord, Lord," yet fail to do as He says, how *can* He save us?

Our only real security in life is found in Jesus' words. As we hear His words and act upon them, we find that obedience to Jesus literally creates a shelter of divine protection. Jesus said,

> "Therefore everyone who hears these words of Mine and acts on them, may be compared to a wise man who built his house on the rock. And the rain fell, and the floods came, and the winds blew and slammed against that house; and yet it did not fall, for it had been founded on the rock.
>
> "Everyone who hears these words of Mine and does not act on them, will be like a foolish man who built his house on the sand. The rain fell, and the floods came, and the winds blew and slammed against that house; and it fell – and great was its fall."   —Matthew 7:24–27

He did not say "if" a storm arises, or "if" by chance the rain should fall – He says *when* the storm comes, *when* the rains fall. Everyone in this world will face storms at certain times of their lives. Listen very carefully: *You cannot build your house in a storm.* Your house must be built day by day, beforehand, by giving yourself to what Jesus says. There *is* a storm on the horizon; do not let this present prosperity deceive you. The only safe place any church is going to have is to dig deep and build on the rock of hearing and obeying the words of Christ.

The Gospel of the Kingdom

In the last days deception will be rampant in the earth. "False Christs and false prophets will arise and will show great signs and wonders, so as to mislead, if possible, even the elect" (Matt. 24:24). We dare not take Jesus' warning casually. His very words are a safeguard for us from the great deception and confusion in our world today.

Yet, in the midst of the warnings of this chapter, Jesus highlights one verse that is the sum of our vision, the very heart of our understanding of truth. He says, "This gospel of the kingdom shall be preached in the whole world." This gospel, which is nothing less than *all* of Jesus' words, is to be proclaimed as a witness in holiness and power, meekness and authority. "And then the end will come" (Matt. 24:14).

God's intention is that the nations see Jesus in us in mercy before they see Christ in the skies in judgment. This is both our hope and vision, that Jesus will be so revealed in us that God could truly be justified in bringing the Great Tribulation to the world when it rejects the likeness of Christ in the church.

If you hear anyone teach that which is inconsistent with the gospel of Jesus Christ, you have a moral obligation, in meekness, to present your concern to that teacher. There is no shortcut to reaching the fullness of God's kingdom. It costs our all to obtain God's best. It takes us straight to the cross, then through it. At the cost of our self-life we find the divine life. To this we are called and challenged: to walk according to the gospel of the kingdom!

Let's pray: *Jesus, Your Word I have treasured in my heart; I hunger for Your Word more than my necessary food. Give me grace that I would cherish every word that proceeded from Your mouth. Holy Spirit, fill the words of Christ as I read them, that I would truly be His disciple.*

—Previously unpublished

SELF TEST, CHAPTER FOUR

Remember, we are looking for answers that correspond with this train-
ing. Please write out your answers, allowing the Holy Spirit to provoke
your thoughts. You may want to use them for group discussion. Note:
we do not provide answers to questions you write out. To check your
multiple choice answers, see answer key in the next session.

Chapter 4, Question #1: Describe the relationship
between the Holy Spirit and the Word of God in
transforming your life.

1. Many people want to be saved *from* God. They don't
   really want _____ with the words of God.
   a. connection
   b. intimacy
   c. communication
   d. problems

2. Jesus' words are for:
   a. the Millennium
   b. the first century
   c. all time, including now
   d. the Jews

3. When Jesus gives you something that seems
   impossible, He provides:
   a. rules
   b. grace
   c. directions
   d. a map

4. It is the intense desire of the heart of the Father that
   we would:
   a. forsake human ideas
   b. forsake gimmicks
   c. listen to Jesus
   d. all the above

5. If we do God's Word, it will save us. If we reject His
   Word, it will _____ us (John 12:47–48).
   a. quicken
   b. judge
   c. search
   d. divide

6. You cannot build your house in a storm; it must be
   built:
   a. later
   b. with bricks
   c. with straw
   d. day by day, beforehand

QUOTE:

"You will never have a
greater meeting
with God
than when He comes
living and breathing
through the Scriptures
into your heart.
At that moment
the very same Spirit
that hovered
over creation
in the beginning
is hovering over you,
transforming you into
the image of Christ
through the Word."

7. Our proclamation of the gospel should be in:
   a. holiness
   b. power
   c. meekness and authority
   d. all the above

8. There is no shortcut to reaching the fullness of God's kingdom. To obtain God's best, it costs our:
   a. tithe
   b. all
   c. offering
   d. incense

SESSION THREE:

THE ESCHATOLOGY
OF CHRIST'S FULLNESS

He made known to us the mystery of His will ... with a view to an administration suitable to the fullness of the times, that is, the summing up of all things in Christ, things in the heavens and things on the earth. —*Ephesians 1:9–10*

SESSION THREE AUDIO MESSAGES:

3a. Hopelessness or Vision
3b. With Unveiled Face

Lessons are to be distributed from
the Training Center only, please.

ANSWER KEY TO LAST SESSION'S
SELF TEST QUESTIONS:

CHAPTER THREE. Keeping Your Way Pure
1.d, 2.b, 3.c, 4.b, 5.c, 6.b, 7.d.

CHAPTER FOUR. Devoted to Jesus' Words
1.b, 2.c, 3.b, 4.d, 5.b, 6.d, 7.d, 8.b.

CHAPTER FIVE

WHEN THE CROP PERMITS

Certainly the period prior to Christ's return will be both difficult and perilous. Scripture warns that God's voice will shake all things, things in the heavens and things on the earth (Heb. 12:26). Everything that can be shaken will be shaken and removed (v. 27).

Yet there is more on the calendar of God than increasing judgments and the Rapture. Between now and the Second Coming there will also be a significant, though still partial, re-establishing of God's kingdom in the earth (Dan. 2:44; Matt. 13; Matt. 24:14). A spiritually mature people will serve as the vanguard of His return. Before the Lord is glorified in the earth, He shall be glorified in the church (Isa. 60:1–3; Eph. 5:27). Indeed, the attainment of Christlike maturity in those who pursue the Lord shall not be a mere sidebar on the list of end-time events; it will be the main attraction.

Listen carefully to what Jesus taught. He said,

"The kingdom of God is like a man who casts seed upon the soil; and he goes to bed at night and gets up by day, and the seed sprouts and grows – how, he himself does not know. The soil produces crops by itself; first the blade, then the head, then the mature grain in the head. But when the crop permits, he immediately puts in the sickle, because the harvest has come."

—Mark 4:26–29

Jesus likened the kingdom of God to a farmer waiting for the maturing of His crops. During the harvest season, farmers are concerned about two primary things: the quantity and quality of the harvest. I lived in eastern Iowa. Some corn and soybean fields, which may have started strong, fail or are stunted due to unusually high or low temperatures or lack of rain. As a result, farmers plow under their fields because their crops did not reach maturity. There was no "mature grain in the head."

Just as the farmer will not harvest without the grain becoming mature, so God is seeking a crop of Christ-followers who have reached spiritual maturity. God is after full stature, not just full numbers. Take note: Jesus said, "when the *crop* permits," God puts in the sickle. The return of Christ isn't about a certain "day or hour," for it is the spiritual stature of the harvest that triggers the great unfolding of end-time events. You see, God is not looking at His watch; He's looking at His crop.

What does spiritual maturity look like? Recall Paul's words. He wrote, "We are ready to punish all disobedience, whenever your obedience is complete" (2 Cor. 10:6). What does complete obedience look like? It looks like Christians taking "every thought captive to the obedience of Christ" (2 Cor. 10:5). Again, God is looking for Christlikeness to ripen within us as we approach the end of the age. Indeed, our maturing can actually hasten the coming of the day of the Lord (2 Pet. 3:12).

"Man ... in the image of God" is the seed-idea purposed by the Almighty from before time began (Gen. 1:27). It does not in any way mean we think we are gods or that we take Christ's place; it means precisely that Christ has truly taken our place: He takes our place at the cross; He takes our place in intercessory prayer, and He takes our place on earth by the manifestation of His will and presence through us (Gal. 2:20). This is the original plan before the world was created. Adam was not the prototype – Christ is. This is what the "mature grain in the head" looks like: mature Christlikeness.

For too long we have assumed that only the numeric size of the harvest was the focus of the Father. Certainly the number of people saved is pivotal: "the fullness of the Gentiles" must come into the kingdom (Rom. 11:25). However, the Almighty does not just want numbers; He wants spiritual maturity.

Thus, the Lord is not looking at a calendar thinking, "Oh, it's the year 2013 (or 2020, etc.). I have to destroy the world on that date." No. A farmer does not reap his crops without first walking his fields, holding samples of the grain, and studying the maturity and integrity of the seed head before he begins his harvest. Again, the maturity of the crop determines the day of the harvest.

So many Christians are frozen in spiritual immaturity. They are easily offended, often distracted and without prayer or spiritual discipline. We think God is requiring of us simply to hang on, yet the Lord is looking for more. Paul says the goal of God in the church is that "we all attain to the unity of the faith, and of the knowledge of the Son of God, to a *mature man*, to the measure of the stature which belongs to the fullness of Christ" (Eph. 4:13, *italics mine*).

Even now, believers around the world are becoming increasingly more Christlike. They live in India and China, Africa and South America, Europe and North America, and places beyond. Yes, they are comparatively a little flock, yet "with unveiled face" they are "beholding as in a mirror the glory of the Lord" and "are being transformed into the same image from glory to glory" (2 Cor. 3:18). When this crop permits, the Father shall put in His sickle, for the harvest has come.

MATURE LABORERS FOR A LARGE HARVEST!

So, the Lord seeks Christlike maturity in His elect. And He does indeed seek for the lost to come into His kingdom. Beloved, I fear that too many Christians are looking to be raptured instead of looking for the reaping. I, too, long to be united with Jesus. Yet, regardless where we stand on the Rapture, whether pre-, mid- or post-Tribulation, the reaping of the nations, according to Scripture, must precede the Rapture. We can be pre-Tribulation in our view, but post-harvest concerning the time of the Rapture.

Look at Matthew thirteen. Jesus again taught of the great season of ingathering. He said,

> "The field is the world; and as for the good seed, these are the sons of the kingdom; and the tares are the sons of the evil one; and the enemy who sowed them is the devil, and the harvest is the end of the age."
> —Matthew 13:38–39

The harvest is not the Rapture. It may be consummated in the Rapture ("gather the wheat into my barn," v. 30), but the process of preparation – sowing, cultivation, and watering – begins long before the crop is cut and finally gathered into the barn at season's end.

In verse 30, Jesus explains, "Allow both [wheat and tares] to grow together until the harvest."

Remember, "the harvest is at the end of the age" and "the field is the world." In the field (the world) tares and wheat grow side by side until the harvest. In other words, the harvest includes "wheat" people growing side by side with "tare" people in "every nation, people, tribe and tongue" when the Rapture occurs. My point is, nearly thirty percent of the world has no wheat growing in it at all, much less wheat growing together with tares!

The seed has yet to be sown in most of China, India, Pakistan – well over two billion people in these three countries alone! Yet Jesus' vision included the whole world with wheat and tares growing together. How can we expect the Rapture at any minute when thirty percent of the world has never heard the good news?

Remember also, Jesus said, "This gospel of the kingdom shall be preached in the whole world as a testimony to all the nations, <u>and then the end will come</u>" (Matt. 24:14).

If we consider prayerfully and humbly that the gospel must be preached in "the whole world" and "to all the nations," and that worldwide the wheat will be growing alongside tares until the season of harvest, we will discover that mankind is not ready yet for God to put in the sickle. The harvest is yet to come.

As maturing Christians, are we thinking, planning, praying about this harvest? Every living church ought to have a strong vision for missions. Even if we are not the ones being sent, we should make it part of our daily prayer to "beseech the Lord of the harvest to send out laborers into His harvest" (Luke 10:2).

Many Christians think God is only concerned about Western nations. We suffer from the same narrow, cultural pride that blinded the early Jewish Christians. They were reluctant to welcome the Gentiles into the harvest; we are ready to eliminate the Chinese, Indian and Muslim worlds.

<u>But the Father must be true to His heart, not our selective expectations. God so loved the *world*.</u> Jesus died for the sins of the *world*. The Lord desires "<u>all men to be saved</u>" (1 Tim. 2:3–4).

POURED OUT ON ALL FLESH

"And it shall be in the last days," God says, "That I will pour forth of My Spirit on all mankind" (Acts 2:17). Today, the Lord desires to pour out the Holy Spirit on all nations, not just our familiar, smaller worlds. Indeed, according to the World Prayer Center in Colorado Springs, more people have been born again into the kingdom of God in the last ten years than the total of all those saved since the time of Christ!

We are in the season of harvest but not yet at the final act of the harvest, the Rapture. Nations will be shaken and disciplined as God prepares all peoples for the gospel. The Lord God has two things He intends to accomplish before the end comes: In *every* nation God will have a people who are living side by side with the "tares," causing them to ripen into the character of Christ. And when this crop permits, the Lord will immediately put in His sickle, for the harvest has come.

Let's pray: *Lord Jesus, as You continue looking for spiritual completeness in the harvest, help me to grow to full stature, that I may truly represent a planting that has grown up into Your likeness.*

—FROM PASTOR FRANGIPANE'S EMAIL TEACHING

SELF TEST, CHAPTER FIVE

Remember, we are looking for answers that correspond with this training. Please write out your answers, allowing the Holy Spirit to provoke your thoughts. You may want to use them for group discussion. Note: we do not provide answers to questions you write out. To check your multiple choice answers, see answer key in the next session.

Chapter 5, Question #1: A harvest is measured by two values – both in the quantity of seeds harvested and their quality. If God is, in fact, expecting maturity from the seed He planted in our lives, how does that encourage you?

1. Just as the farmer will not harvest without the grain becoming mature, so God is seeking a crop of Christ-followers who have:
   a. little sprouts
   b. been plowed under
   c. been uprooted
   d. reached spiritual maturity

2. This is what the "mature grain in the head" looks like:
   a. corn
   b. mature Christlikeness
   c. a mustard seed
   d. John the Baptist

3. Many Christians are frozen in spiritual immaturity. They are:
   a. easily offended
   b. often distracted
   c. without prayer or spiritual discipline
   d. all the above

4. "The harvest is at the end of the age" and "the field is the _____":
   a. baseball diamond
   b. world
   c. sugar cane
   d. soil

5. "This gospel of the kingdom shall be preached in the _____ as a testimony to all the nations, and then the end will come" (Matt. 24:14).
   a. whole world
   b. street
   c. pulpit
   d. church

6. Every living church ought to have a strong vision for missions. We should "beseech the Lord of the harvest to send out laborers _____" (Luke 10:2).
   a. for more services
   b. to paint the church basement
   c. into His harvest
   d. to labor

7. We must not have the narrow cultural pride that blinded the early Jewish Christians. The Lord desires "_____ men to be saved" (I Tim. 2:4):
   a. some
   b. all
   c. short
   d. old men

8. We are in the season of harvest but not yet at the final act of the harvest, the _____:
   a. tilling
   b. Rapture
   c. sowing
   d. picking

QUOTE:

"Even now, believers around the world are becoming increasingly more Christlike … They are comparatively a little flock, yet 'with unveiled face' they are 'beholding … the glory of the Lord' and 'are being transformed into the same image [of Christ] from glory to glory.'
(2 Cor. 3:18)."

CHAPTER SIX

THE INTENSIFYING PRESENCE

We all know the unrepentant world is destined for the Great Tribulation, but as far as the living, praying church is concerned, if we continue to climb toward the standard of Christlikeness, prior to the Rapture there will be a season of great glory for true Christians.

In support of this holy goal, let me submit to you an encounter I had with the Lord in 1973. I was pastoring a small church in Hawaii and had been in a month of intense prayer and extended fasting, a time of drawing near to God. At the end of this period, I found myself awakened during the night by a visitation of the Lord. It was not as though I saw His physical features; I saw His glory and was overwhelmed by the intense fire of His presence.

Immediately I was like a dead man, unable to move so much as a finger. Spiritually, however, my consciousness was heightened beyond anything I have known since. I felt like one of those "living creatures" in the book of Revelation with "eyes around and within" (Rev. 4:8).

With my "inner eyes" I saw the truth about my personal righteousness. Recall, I had been in prayer and fasting; I felt good about myself. Yet, suddenly, the flaws in my life became unbearably vivid and utterly sinful. My iniquity was not as something I occasionally committed but as something I perpetually was. I saw many times when I could have been more loving or kind or sensitive. I also saw how selfish nearly all of my actions were.

Yet for all that was dark within me, I felt no rebuke from the Lord nor condemnation. No voice came from Heaven to convict me of my wrongs. The only voice condemning me was my own; in the light of His presence, I abhorred myself (Job 42:6 KJV).

Without any buffer of self-justification or deceit, I saw how far short of His glory I truly was. I knew why mankind needed the blood of Christ, and no amount of personal attainment in and of itself could ever make me like Jesus. In the most profound way I understood that only Christ could live like Christ. God's plan was not to improve me but to remove me so that the Lord Jesus Himself could actually live His life through me (Gal. 2:20). In His indwelling would rest my hope of becoming like Him.

Outwardly, with "eyes around," I realized that the electrified atmosphere I felt in my bedroom was actually being broadcast from a very distant reality. Yet, though distant, the emanation of Christ's presence was like a burning fire upon my consciousness. A great procession of heavenly beings was descending through a night sky; I knew that this was a glimpse of Heaven coming to earth.

In the forefront were angels of every class and order, each group in a splendor all its own. About one third of the way back was the Lord, and behind Him were innumerable saints. Yet I could not see into the depth of the Lord's glory, for those following Him had become part of His being.

The Lord was not only coming to judge the earth but to fill this world with His glory. Let me repeat that, even though the Lord was far away, the radiance of His presence was like a living fire upon my consciousness. The energy was almost painful.

..Because there was . fire in my hand.

Then, without warning, the procession came closer, not just to me but to our dimension. It was as though a mark in time had been crossed. Instantly I was utterly overwhelmed by the intensity of the Lord's presence. I felt that I could not – no, not for another moment – bear the increase of His glory. It was as though my very existence would be consumed by the blast furnace of His radiance. And in the deepest prayer I have ever uttered, I begged the Lord to return me to my body. Instantly, mercifully, I was cocooned once again in the familiar world of my senses and my bedroom.

What It Means

Night passed into dawn and I rose early, dressed, and went outside. With each step, I pondered the vision. The Lord brought my attention to the sun as it ascended above the eastern horizon. As I looked, I saw parallels between the radiance of the sunlight and the glory of the Lord. I realized in a new way that "the heavens are telling of the glory of God" (Ps. 19:1).

I saw that even though the sun is 93 million miles from the earth, we feel its heat and live in its light. It is inconceivably far away, yet its energy is also here. It warms us and in its light our life exists. So also the expanse of the Lord's presence emanates from His glorified body in Heaven. Physically He is distant, yet at times we actually feel the outraying of His presence here; we are, in truth, warmed by His love.

The glory of Christ, like the outraying of the sun, is "safe" as long as He remains distant from us in Heaven. But imagine if, with each successive decade, the sun were to steadily move closer to the earth. Radiation, heat, and light would increase dramatically. With each stage of its approach, the world as we know it would radically change!

So also will this world change spiritually as the person of the Lord Jesus and His millennial reign draw near. The radiance of His presence will increasingly pour into the spiritual realms surrounding our world. And not only the "powers of the heavens will be shaken" (Matt. 24:29; Heb. 12), but the very world as we know it will experience dramatic changes.

If the sun drew closer, the increasing heat and light would soon be all we would think about. While the righteous are experiencing "glory and honor and peace" from His presence (Rom. 2:10), the same glory will cause terrible "tribulation and distress" to the unrepentant world (v. 9). The wicked will cry to the mountains and rocks: "Fall on us and hide us." But from what? "From the *presence* of [the Lord]" (Rev. 6:16, *italics mine*).

Those hardened in sin will either find grace and repent or their hardness will deepen like Pharaoh's. Yet the same sun that hardens the clay also melts the butter. So, as He draws nearer, the prayer of the righteous will be, *"Fill us with the presence of the Lamb!"* The presence of Christ will be all that fills our minds. Those who love Him will experience the increase of His pleasure; they will taste the nectar of Heaven. Whether we are for or against the Lord, everyone's mind will be flooded with thoughts about God.

As it is written,

"For behold, the day is coming, burning like a furnace; and all the arrogant and every evildoer will be chaff; and the day that is coming will set them ablaze," says the Lord of hosts, "so that it will leave them neither root nor branch.

"But for you who fear My name, the sun of righteousness will rise with healing in its wings; and you will go forth and skip about like calves from the stall.

"You will tread down the wicked, for they shall be ashes under the soles of your feet on the day which I am preparing," says the Lord of hosts.   —Malachi 4:1–3

Simultaneously two events will manifest on earth; they will be the result of one eternal source. The same increasing presence will cause wrath to descend upon the wicked and God's glory to be seen upon the righteous. For we who fear the Lord, the "sun of righteousness" will rise with healing in its rays.

SAME JESUS, NEW SPLENDOR

When Christ returns to this world, He is coming clothed in the splendor of the Father (Mark 8:38). My prayer is that each of us will perceive this reality: it is *God* Himself who is drawing near to earth! The prophet, Habakkuk, gives us an awesome view into the actual day when the Lord reveals Himself to the world. He wrote:

> God comes from Teman, and the Holy One from Mount Paran. Selah. His splendor covers the heavens, and the earth is full of His praise. His radiance is like the sunlight; He has rays flashing from His hand, and there is the hiding of His power.
> —Habakkuk 3:3–4

There will be a time when the Lord Jesus actually is revealed in the heavens. In that final moment His splendor will literally flood the skies like "the sunlight." Every eye will see Him with power flashing like terrible bolts of lightning from His hands.

Yet, *before He appears,* while He is near but still invisible, that same radiance of glory will be poured out on "all flesh" (Acts 2:17–21). For as He is in power and glory when He appears, so He is beforehand though unseen! And it is this outraying presence that will grow ever more resplendent in the church prior to His second coming.

With each surge of His glory many things will be quickened on earth. Satan, and the nations under him, will rage against the Lord and His purposes. Demonically manipulated social and ethnic upheaval will intensify, increasing lawlessness, rebellion, and hopelessness in the world. The earth itself will suffer as droughts, and air and water pollution, cause unpredictable and, in many cases, disastrous changes in the patterns of life. There will be earthquakes in regions where earthquakes were unknown. Coastal cities will have mass evacuations, for there will be "dismay among nations, in perplexity at the roaring of the sea and the waves" (Luke 21:25).

At the same time, we who are open and yielded to Christ will watch in amazement as His presence *in us* also intensifies and increases! He will invade our thoughts, plunder our unbelief, and purge our carnality. He will present to Himself a bride without spot or wrinkle or any such thing.

The church will be beautified with His glory and filled with His radiance *before* He physically comes for her! A time will come when our repentance and reconciliation will be complete. At that time the Scripture will be fulfilled that the bride of Christ "has made herself ready" (Rev. 19:7). The church will find in Christ a new level of holiness and purity, which will manifest in a radiance that is both "bright and clean" (v. 8).

Many promises given to the church, formerly thought impossible, will be fulfilled by the fullness of Christ in us. The days ahead will be seasons of glory. The Shekinah presence of Christ, as He is enthroned upon the praises of His people, will manifest and abide in unfading glory. We have not yet seen worship services like those that await us in the future. The day is coming when the command of the worship leaders shall be to "make His praise glorious"! (Ps. 66:2). A spiritual majesty will accompany the worshippers of God. Even among the most simple peoples of earth, those who love God will be companioned by His royal presence.

In the most profound ways, the magnificence of the Lord will unfold before us. We will marvel at how God has humbled and brought low the kings of the earth. But one King shall ever rise in prominence. To Him every knee will bow! And while we too shall bow at His splendor, our highest joy shall be that we have personally known Him!

As each new level of glory arrives and unfolds, the Holy Spirit will require fresh and frequent examinations of our relationship with Christ. Whether our backgrounds are evangelical or charismatic, traditional or Pentecostal, *all who love the Lord will change.* For whatever inhibits the fusion of our lives with Christ will be consumed like chaff in the fire of His presence.

In this season of transformation, we will know Him both in the fellowship of His sufferings and in the power of His resurrection. We will know the fullness of Christ. And it shall come to pass – not because of our righteousness but because of His increasing fullness. He *must* increase and we *must* decrease until His presence fills everything, everywhere, with Himself.

Let's pray: *Father, I am staggered by the promise of obtaining Christ's glory! I am filled with awe and holy fear. Even as I study and pray, I realize You are actually transforming my heart. Oh, God, fill me with Your living presence. May the vision of possessing Your glory become the single compelling joy of my life!*

—FROM THE BOOK *THE DAYS OF HIS PRESENCE*

SELF TEST, CHAPTER SIX

Remember, we are looking for answers that correspond with this training. Please write out your answers, allowing the Holy Spirit to provoke your thoughts. You may want to use them for group discussion. Note: we do not provide answers to questions you write out. To check your multiple choice answers, see answer key in the next session.

Chapter 6, Question #1: If it is true that among the elect there will be an increasing awareness of the Lord's presence at the end of the age, how does that reconfigure your priorities?
How does that impact your focus?

1. The surest way to know God is by:
   a. studying His Word
   b. watching TV
   c. socializing
   d. listening to tapes

2. If we continue to climb toward the standard of Christlikeness, ahead of us lies a time of:
   a. waiting
   b. great glory
   c. harvest
   d. both b & c

3. In Pastor Francis' encounter with the Lord in 1973, he realized that the only voice condemning him was his own, not the Lord's. He understood that only Christ could:
   a. live like Christ
   b. attend weekly church services
   c. give us permission to work
   d. provide "some" of what we need

4. During that visitation, he understood that God's plan was not to improve us but to:
   a. condemn us
   b. condition us
   c. remove us so He could live through us
   d. bend us

5. The Lord is not just coming to judge the earth but to:
   a. make us wealthy
   b. shake the earth
   c. spin the earth the other way
   d. fill this world with His glory

6. While the righteous will experience "glory and honor and peace" from His presence (Rom. 2:10), the same glory will cause:
   a. terrible tribulation and distress
   b. confusion
   c. a mild headache
   d. joy

7. Before the Lord appears, while He is near but still invisible, that same radiance of glory will be poured out _____ (Acts 2:17–21).
   a. from tiny buckets in Heaven
   b. only on those from our particular church
   c. on "all flesh"
   d. like water

8. The bride of Christ will be beautified with Christ's glory and filled with His radiance _____ the Lord physically comes for her.
   a. as soon as
   b. after
   c. before
   d. when

Session Four:

Revealing Christ

in Suffering

For we who live are constantly being delivered over to death for Jesus' sake, so that the life of Jesus also may be manifested in our mortal flesh.

—2 Corinthians 4:11

SESSION FOUR AUDIO MESSAGES:

4a. The Gift of Woundedness
4b. The Perfection of Love

Lessons are to be distributed from
the Training Center only, please.

ANSWER KEY TO LAST SESSION'S
SELF TEST QUESTIONS:

CHAPTER FIVE. When the Crop Permits
1.d, 2.b, 3.d, 4.b, 5.a, 6.c, 7.b, 8.b.

CHAPTER SIX. The Intensifying Presence
1.a, 2.d, 3.a, 4.c, 5.d, 6.a, 7.c, 8.c.

CHAPTER SEVEN

THE GIFT
OF WOUNDEDNESS

The world and all it contains was created for one purpose: to showcase the grandeur of God's Son. In Jesus, the nature of God is magnificently and perfectly revealed; He is the *"express image"* of God (Heb. 1:3 KJV). Yet to gaze upon Christ is also to see God's pattern for man. As we seek to be like Him, we discover that our need was created for His sufficiency. We also see that, once the redemptive nature of Christ begins to triumph in our lives, mercy begins to triumph in the world around us.

How will we recognize revival when it comes? Behold, here is the awakening we seek: men and women, young and old, all conformed to Jesus. When will revival begin? It starts the moment we say "yes" to becoming like Him; it spreads to others as Christ is revealed through us.

Yet to embrace Christ's attitude toward mercy is but a first step in our spiritual growth. The process of being truly conformed to Christ compels us into deeper degrees of transformation. Indeed, just as Jesus learned obedience through the things that He suffered (Heb. 5:8), so also must we. And it is here, even while we stand in intercession or service to God, that Christ gives us the *gift* of woundedness.

"Gift?" you ask. Yes, to be wounded in the service of mercy and, instead of closing our hearts, allow woundedness to crown love, is to release God's power in redemption. The steadfast prayer of the wounded intercessor holds great sway upon the heart of God.

We cannot become Christlike without being wounded. You see, even after we come to Christ, we carry encoded within us preset limits concerning how far we will go for love, and how much we are willing to suffer for redemption. When God allows us to be wounded, He exposes those human boundaries and reveals what we lack of His nature.

The path narrows as we seek true transformation. Indeed, many Christians fall short of Christ's stature because they have been hurt and offended by people. They leave churches discouraged, vowing never again to serve or lead or contribute because, when they offered themselves, their gift was marred by unloving people. To be struck or rejected in the administration of mercy can become a great offense to us, especially as we are waiting for, and even expecting, a reward for our good efforts.

Yet wounding is inevitable if we are following Christ. Jesus was both "marred" (Isa. 52:14) and "wounded" (Zech. 13:6), and if we are sincere in our pursuit of His nature, we will suffer as well. How else will love be perfected?

Let us beware. We either become Christlike and forgive the offenders or we enter a spiritual time warp where we abide continually in the memory of our wounding. Like a systemic disease, the hurtful memories infect every aspect of our existence. In truth, apart from God, the wounding that life inflicts is incurable. God has decreed that only Christ in us can survive.

Intercessors live on the frontier of change. We are positioned to stand between the needs of man and the provision of God. Because we are the agents of redemption, Satan will always seek the means to offend, discourage, silence, or otherwise steal the strength of our prayers. The wounding we receive must be interpreted in light of God's promise to reverse the effects of evil and make injustice work for our good (Rom. 8:28). Since spiritual assaults are inevitable, we must discover how God uses our wounds as the means to greater power. This was exactly how Christ brought redemption to the world.

Jesus knew that maintaining love and forgiveness in the midst of suffering was the key that unlocked the power of redemption. Isaiah 53:11 tells us, "By His knowledge the Righteous One, My Servant, will justify the many, as He will bear their iniquities."

Jesus possessed revelation knowledge into the mystery of God. He knew that the secret to unleashing world-transforming power was found at the cross, in suffering. At the cross, payment for sin was made. As Christ forgave His enemies, Heaven's power rent the temple veil in two. Christ's stripes purchased our healing. I am not just talking about suffering, but the suffering of love.

The terrible offense of the cross became the place of redemption for the world. Yet, remember, Jesus calls us to a cross as well (Matt. 16:24). Wounding is simply an altar upon which our sacrifice to God is prepared.

Listen again to Isaiah's prophetic description of Jesus' life. His words, at first, seem startling, but as we read, we discover a most profound truth concerning the power of woundedness. He wrote,

But the Lord was pleased to crush Him, putting Him to grief; if He would render Himself as a guilt offering, He will see His offspring, He will prolong His days, and the good pleasure of the Lord will prosper in His hand.   —Isaiah 53:10

How did the power of God's pleasure prosper in Christ's hand? During His times of crushing, woundedness and devastation, instead of retaliating, Jesus rendered Himself "as a guilt offering."

The crushing is not a disaster; it is an opportunity. You see, our purposeful love may or may not touch the sinner's heart, but it always touches the heart of God. We are crushed by people, but we need to allow the crushing to ascend as an offering to God. The greatest benefit of all is the effect our mercy has on the Father. If we truly want to be instruments of God's good pleasure, then it is redemption, not wrath, that must prosper in our hands. If we are Christ-followers, we must offer ourselves as an offering for the guilt of others.

CONFORMED TO THE LAMB

When Christ encounters conflict, though He is the Lion of Judah, He comes as the Lamb of God. Even when He is outwardly stern, His heart is always mindful that He is the "guilt offering." Thus, Jesus not only asks the Father to forgive those who have wounded Him, but also numbers Himself with the transgressors and intercedes for them (Isa. 53:12). He does this because the Father takes "no pleasure in the death of the wicked" (Ezek. 33:11), and it is the pleasure of God that Jesus seeks.

Is this not the wonder and mystery – yes, and the power – of Christ's cross? In anguish and sorrow, wounded in heart and soul, still He offered Himself for His executioners' sins. Without visible evidence of success, deemed a sinner and a failure before man, He courageously held true to mercy. In the depth of terrible crushing, He let love attain its most glorious perfection. He uttered the immortal words, "Father, forgive them; for they do not know what they are doing" (Luke 23:34).

Christ could have escaped. He told Peter as the Romans came to arrest Him, "Do you think that I cannot appeal to My Father, and He will at once put at My disposal more than twelve legions of angels?" (Matt. 26:53). In less than a heartbeat, the skies would have been flooded with thousands of warring angels. Yes, Jesus could have escaped, but mankind would have perished. Christ chose to go to hell for us rather than return to Heaven without us. Instead of condemning mankind, He rendered *"Himself* as a guilt offering" (Isa. 53:10, *italics mine).* He prayed the mercy prayer, *"Father, forgive them"* (Luke 23:34).

Jesus said, "He who believes in Me, the works that I do, he will do also" (John 14:12). We assume He meant that we would work His miracles, but Jesus did not limit His definition of "works" to the miraculous. The works He did – the redemptive life, the mercy cry, the identification with sinners, rendering Himself a guilt offering – *all* the works He did, we will *"do also."*

Thus, because He lives within us, we see that Isaiah 53 does not apply exclusively to Jesus; it also becomes the blueprint for Christ in us. Indeed, was this not part of His reward, that "He [would] see His offspring"? (Isa. 53:10). Beloved, *we* are the progeny of Christ!

Read these words from Paul's heart:

Now I rejoice in my sufferings for your sake, and in my flesh I do my share on behalf of His body, which is the church, in filling up what is lacking in Christ's afflictions.　　　　　—Colossians 1:24

What did the apostle mean? Did not Christ fully pay mankind's debts once and for all? Did

Paul imply that *we* now take *Jesus'* place? No, we will never take Jesus' place. It means that Jesus has come to take our place. The Son of God manifests all the aspects of His redemptive, sacrificial life through us. Indeed, "as He is, so also are we in this world" (1 John 4:17).

Paul not only identified with Christ in his personal salvation, but he was also consumed with Christ's purpose. He wrote, "That I may know Him and the power of His resurrection and the fellowship of His sufferings, being conformed to His death" (Phil. 3:10).

What a wondrous reality is the "fellowship of His sufferings." Here, in choosing to yoke our existence with Christ's purpose, we find true friendship with Jesus. This is intimacy with Christ. The sufferings of Christ are not the sorrows typically endured by mankind; they are the afflictions of love. They bring us closer to Jesus. We learn how precious is the gift of woundedness.

Let's pray: *Father, I see You have had no other purpose in my life but to manifest through me the nature of Your Son. I receive the gift of woundedness. In response, in surrender to Christ, I render myself an offering for those You've used to crush me. May the fragrance of my worship remind You of Jesus, and may You forgive, sprinkle and cleanse the world around me.*

—FROM THE BOOK *THE POWER OF ONE CHRISTLIKE LIFE*

SELF TEST, CHAPTER SEVEN

Remember, we are looking for answers that correspond with this training. Please write out your answers, allowing the Holy Spirit to provoke your thoughts. You may want to use them for group discussion. Note: we do not provide answers to questions you write out. To check your multiple choice answers, see answer key in the next session.

Chapter 7, Question #1: Have you been wounded by people even as you sought to serve Christ? How can you reverse the effects of injustice in your life and use the very wounding of your heart to perfect Christ's love through you?

1. As we seek the fullness of Christ, we discover that:
   a. it's absolutely not going to happen
   b. our need was created for His sufficiency
   c. all we really need to become is nice people
   d. there is no way

2. Once the redemptive nature of Christ begins to triumph in our lives, mercy begins to:
   a. fade
   b. triumph through us into the world around us
   c. look for a means to escape
   d. live

3. It is through woundedness that love will be:
   a. destroyed
   b. lost
   c. perfected
   d. squished

4. Jesus knew that maintaining _____ and _____ in the midst of suffering unjustly was the key that unlocked the power of redemption.
   a. Bible study and discussion
   b. gossip and jogging
   c. spiritual gossip & exercise
   d. love and forgiveness

5. Crushing is not a disaster. It is an:
   a. event
   b. opportunity
   c. episode
   d. exercise

6. In John 14:12 Jesus does not limit His works (that we will also do) to miracles. Rather, the works include:
   a. identification with sinners
   b. the mercy cry
   c. rendering ourselves a guilt offering
   d. all the above

7. In Philippians 3:10 we learn that we are not only to be identified with Christ in our personal salvation, but also consumed with:
   a. guilt
   b. Christ's purpose
   c. studying
   d. reading

8. What a wondrous reality is the "fellowship of His sufferings." Here in choosing to yoke our existence with Christ's purpose, we find true:
   a. unity with the Lord
   b. friendship with Jesus
   c. intimacy with Christ
   d. all the above

> **QUOTE:**
>
> *"Jesus not only asks the Father to forgive those who have wounded Him, but also numbers Himself with the transgressors and intercedes for them (Isa. 53:12). He does this because the Father takes 'no pleasure in the death of the wicked' (Ezek. 33:11), and it is the pleasure of God that Jesus seeks."*

CHAPTER SEVEN: THE GIFT OF WOUNDEDNESS

CHAPTER EIGHT

SATAN'S HOUR

There is no greater opportunity to become Christ-like than in the midst of pain and injustice. When Satan is raging with evil, God is planning to turn it to good. If we maintain our integrity in battle, if we let love rise to its purest expression, then we will touch the heart of God. Such is the path to our Father's power.

My prayer is that by embracing Christlikeness we will have eliminated a number of the vulnerabilities to – and effects of – church splits and other ungodly divisions. At the same time, I realize that we can do almost everything right as pastors, leaders and churches and still suffer divisions. For some of us, this may actually be part of God's greater plan for our lives – that we should endure rejection, conflict and slander as part of the process of truly becoming Christlike.

During seasons of conflict, as leaders and leaders-in-training, we must understand how to use battle to become more Christlike.

A COLLECTIVE MADNESS

Let me speak to those who feel strife and division has its place in the church. My earnest admonition is that you flee quickly from a divisive group. If you do not heed my warning and instead fully embrace the resolve to split your church, a type of "collective madness" will occur. You will know what you are doing is wrong but will become so hardened that you detach yourself from guilt. You will be aware that your anger is venomous and unChristlike, but you will be powerless to mute your words.

Beloved, no one needs to slay love to defend truth. Love is not truth's enemy; it is its validator. If what you say cannot be said in love, do not say it. It is not of God. To speak without love is evidence that the collective madness has begun to infect your soul.

A Visitation from Hell

Let us isolate this terrible insanity that drives people to say and do things they know are wrong. For the sake of discernment, we shall call this season of madness "Satan's hour." It is a period of time when the restraining powers of all that is good seem to withdraw from human relationships. Instead of love – or even civility – what governs the dissenting group is the manifest "power of darkness" (Luke 22:53). It is as though people invite the legions of hell to depart the abode of the damned and find access to their secret resentments – the unresolved issues that exist in their hearts. Those things that are evil within human nature are fully awakened and then empowered by hell to fulfill every demonic gratification.

This collective madness is the exact opposite of a visitation from Heaven; it is a visitation from hell. It is not the healing of bodies but the wounding of hearts. It is not reconciliation between souls but estrangement of friends. It is not truth spoken in love but emotions discharged in wrath. It is not the gospel of peace but the heartache of strife. During Satan's hour friends become enemies, loyalties become betrayals and unity degrades into irreconcilable division. Satan's hour is an uncontested, seemingly unstoppable, invasion from hell where every hidden jealousy and every secret unresolved bitterness in the human heart is unsheathed and used as a weapon in the hands of demons of strife.

During His last few days on earth, Jesus Himself watched this invasion from hell advance upon the people of Jerusalem, infecting even His own disciples. If we study the terrible, demonic events that were compressed into Jesus' final earthly days, we gain vital insight into the demonic activity in church splits. And more importantly we can see how God can bring victory through it.

WHAT JESUS ENDURED

This swarm of evil did not take Jesus unaware. Throughout His ministry Jesus frequently warned His disciples that a time of unfettered evil would come (Mark 8:31, 9:12; Luke 17:25). As the day arrived, Jesus announced to His disciples that the hour of darkness was at hand (John 14:30). Knowing a time of satanic darkness would come did not make it less painful, but having such insight helped Jesus to prepare.

Jesus was fully aware that during Satan's hour evil would strike in full force and His disciples would be sifted severely (Luke 22:31). He knew His followers would scatter, and one of the twelve would betray Him. Indeed, even His closest friends would deny they ever knew Him (Luke 22:60–61). Satan's hour was a time when reality itself seemingly bent in service to the power of darkness (Luke 22:53), and the Father offered nothing Jesus could use to stop it.

We cannot help but picture Jesus always upbeat and overcoming, but when hell was unleashed, even God's Son was not invulnerable to Satan's oppression. "Grieved and distressed," Jesus took His closest friends aside and spoke intimately with them about His heartache (Matt. 26:37).

"My soul is deeply grieved, to the point of death," He said, as He urged His closest friends, Peter, James and John, to keep watch with Him. Yet, the heaviness of satanic battle overwhelmed them. Even John, who had rested his head on Jesus' breast, could not lift his head from slumber. All escaped into sleep, hiding themselves from excessive sorrow (Matt. 26:38–45).

Staggered by the weight of the spiritual attack against Him, Jesus "fell to the ground and began to pray that if it were possible, the hour might pass Him by" (Mark 14:35). We know Jesus ministered peace wherever He went, yet now His intense, internal struggle ruptured blood vessels on His face, which beaded on His skin. Again He sought to waken His disciples. Roused from their sleep, they saw the droplets of blood on His brow and cheeks; still, they could not endure.

I think it is significant that Jesus, so familiar with simply trusting His Father in all things, returned to His friends three times during the hour of His Gethsemane prayer (Matt. 26:39–45). Beloved, there are some agonies in life for which God alone seems not enough; we crave also the comfort of our friends (Prov. 17:17). There is no substitute for God, yet our soul also needs the embrace of a loyal companion, the shoulder of a faithful friend who has become closer than a brother.

Jesus' friends, however, were not there for Him. They slept while He prayed. They fled when the Pharisees came (Matt. 26:56). During the trial when they – of all people – certainly could have defended Jesus' character and doctrine, they hid. Even if others would forsake Him, surely these who broke bread with Him – who knew His heart – would speak in His defense. Yet from Gethsemane to the cross, Jesus heard the voice of just one friend. Peter, who less than a day earlier had sworn undying loyalty, now swore he never knew Him (Matt. 26:69–70; Luke 22:60–61).

Our Master experienced betrayal, abandonment, slander, mockery and gross injustice. He endured the heartache of His disciples' failures – to pray, to stand and to defend the truth about their most wonderful friend and Lord.

Dear follower of Jesus, what our Messiah endured and what the disciples suffered – in various degrees – are all the elements found in a church split. What happens to a pastor or leader – what might have happened to *your* pastor during a church split – is similar in nature to what Jesus Himself suffered in His last few days.

How Jesus Overcame

For a leader, there exists only one way out of the tragedy of a church split: become like Jesus. God's greatest goal for our lives is not that we become successful ministers, but that we become Christlike. Leading is simply an opportunity to be transformed into Christlikeness. This does not mean we must die for the sins of the world, but it does mean that when we go through injustices and conflicts, Christ must be manifested in our mortal lives.

What I mean by "manifesting Christ in our lives" is that we learn to respond to the human failures in our world as Jesus did in His. The wounding that strikes a pastor during a split comes through several sources. One of the worst is the apparent failure of church members and friends to speak in his defense. Confusion, fear and doubt can overshadow a congregation, even those who know better, paralyzing them into inaction. To counteract His disciples' failure, and knowing they, too, were being sifted, Jesus assured them, "But I have prayed for you, that your faith may not fail; and you, when once you have turned again, strengthen your brothers" (Luke 22:32).

There were valuable lessons for Jesus' disciples that only failure could teach, and Jesus knew this. These disciples had been arguing among themselves which of them might be the greatest; now they were humbled, broken and contrite enough for God to use them. God used their failure to excavate their souls of pride; now emptied, they were capable of being filled with the Holy Spirit. These same disciples would soon be willing to suffer and die for Jesus – and count it an honor to do so. They never denied Him again. Knowing they would fail Him, Jesus prayed that during their trial their faith would not fail and, upon returning, they would become a strength for others.

The disciples' greatest problem was carrying the burden of their failure. Their guilt and condemnation weighed heavily upon them. Yet immediately after warning them that they each would, in fact, deny Him, Jesus comforted them: "Let not your heart be troubled" (John 14:1 KJV). Incredibly, even before they fell, Jesus sought to remove the weight of condemnation that would inevitably seek to overwhelm them.

So, friends, as Jesus loved His disciples, even though they failed Him, so we need to love those who, though falling short of our expectations, still remain with us. They will strengthen others. We need to remove any sense of condemnation or blame from those who have disappointed us. As they see our Christlike reactions, they too will become united to serve God's highest purposes.

How Jesus Handled His Enemies

Jesus loved His disciples, and His love brought them through. But what about those people who played the role of the enemy, those who were instruments of injustice, who sought to destroy Jesus' ministry through gossip and slander. We must find Christ's reaction to these and emulate His behavior.

While Jesus had many legitimate arguments to wage against His accusers, He stood silently before them. In this example, Christ shows us that there is a time to take your stand and defend what God is doing, and there is a time to become silent and simply entrust yourself to God. Peter reveals how Jesus processed the storm of accusation that came against His soul. Peter writes, "While being reviled, He did not revile in return; while suffering, He uttered no threats, but kept entrusting Himself to Him who judges righteously" (1 Pet. 2:23). If your words will not persuade your attackers, beloved, recognize it is time to be silent.

Yet Jesus was not just silent. He bore their sins on His cross (1 Pet. 2:24). When facing a storm of accusation, it is not enough that we not react negatively; we must respond positively to those who come against us, just as Christ did. We must pray the mercy prayer, even when it may appear that they have successfully put to death our vision.

You see, Jesus knew Satan's hour was coming. But He also knew that if He could maintain His vision of redemption and His capacity to love, it would be through this very time of darkness that redemption would triumph for mankind. Though grieved and deeply troubled, Jesus prayed, "What shall I say, 'Father, save Me from this hour'? But for this purpose I came" (John 12:27).

Jesus understood that for redemption to be accomplished, His love would face its most severe test. Jesus knew this battle was over one thing: Would He allow love to reach full maturity and its most perfect expression? Would He maintain His passion for man's redemption even as men mocked and crucified Him?

So it is with us. God allows injustices to perfect our love. The cross is the cost we pay so love can triumph. This battle is not about you and your enemies. It is about you choosing to maintain love in the midst of injustice.

Dear follower of Christ, let us redefine our meaning of success. Here is the success that will bring the power of redemption into our world: When we have endured Satan's hour and allowed adversity to refine our love, we will have succeeded in the purpose of our existence.

Beloved, regardless of the test God calls you to endure, it is not about you and your relational opponent. The real issue is about you and God. Will you allow love to be perfected? Will you transform Satan's hour into an offering of your life in Christ-like surrender?

Let's pray: *Lord Jesus, my soul longs and even yearns to be like You. Master of all that is good, grant me grace to succeed in love. Guard my heart from its natural instinct for self-survival. Let me never choose the way of hardness; let me, in all things, find the way of life. Even now, I offer myself for those who have struck me. Thank You for the opportunity to become like You. Amen.*

—FROM THE BOOK *A House United*

SELF TEST, CHAPTER EIGHT

Remember, we are looking for answers that correspond with this training. Please write out your answers, allowing the Holy Spirit to provoke your thoughts. You may want to use them for group discussion. Note: we do not provide answers to questions you write out. To check your multiple choice answers, see answer key in the next session.

Chapter 8, Question #1: If you have ever been involved in a church division or split, in what ways can you become more Christlike because of what you went through?

Chapter 8, Question #2: How does suffering injustice work to make us more Christlike?

1. Part of God's greater plan for our lives may actually be that we should:
   a. endure rejection
   b. never receive injustice
   c. endure slander
   d. both a & c

2. If something cannot be said in love:
  a. try to soften it some
  b. don't say it
  c. be angry but sin not
  d. let 'em have it

3. During "Satan's hour"
  a. friends become enemies
  b. loyalties become betrayals
  c. unity degrades into unreconcilable division
  d. all the above

4. Jesus, so familiar with simply trusting His Father in all things, returned to His friends three times during the hour of His Gethsemane prayer. There are some agonies in life for which:
  a. we crave God AND the comfort of friends
  b. prayer is all we need
  c. there's no comfort
  d. there is no answer

5. What our Messiah endured and what the disciples suffered, in various degrees, are the elements found in:
  a. how-to books
  b. a church split
  c. gardens
  d. groups

6. God's greatest goal for our lives is not that we become successful ministers, but that we become:
  a. great orators
  b. religious
  c. Christlike
  d. rich

7. "Let not your heart be troubled." As Jesus comforted and loved His disciples, even though they failed Him, so it is with those who fall short of our expectations. We need to:
  a. correct them
  b. love and comfort them
  c. isolate them
  d. rebuke them

8. As with Jesus, God allows injustice to:
  a. harm us
  b. perfect our love
  c. make us angry
  d. help us judge

QUOTE:

"For a leader, there exists only one way out of the tragedy of a church split: become like Jesus. God's greatest goal for our lives is not that we become successful ministers, but that we become Christlike. Leading is simply an opportunity to be transformed into Christlikeness."

When...	Jesus...	Likewise, we can...
Jesus knew that this evil aimed at His ministry was coming	Warned His friends (Matt. 17:12, 26:24; Mark 8:31–32,10:33–34; John 14:30)	Prepare those in our care (Acts 20:28–31)
Jesus knew that His friends would be tempted and fail	Prayed for and encouraged them (Luke 22:31–32; John 14:1)	Pray (1 Thess. 5:17) Encourage (Heb. 10:25)
Jesus felt overwhelmed	Admitted His need, asked His friends to pray (Matt. 26:38)	Ask! Paul asks (Heb. 13:18)
Jesus' friends were wearied with excessive sorrow	Encouraged them to remain faithful in prayer (Matt. 26:41)	Encourage (Gal. 6:9)
His enemies accused Jesus	Did not respond in anger (Matt. 26:62–64)	Love enemies (Matt. 5) Entrust to God (1 Pet. 2:23)
Jesus' friends betrayed Him	Forgave and restored them (John 21:15–19)	Forgive (Matt. 6) Restore (Gal. 6:1)
Jesus could not escape unjust suffering	Saw the redemptive hand of His Father behind it (John 12:27)	Imitate Christ (Eph. 5:1–2) Trust (Rom. 8:28)

SESSION FIVE:

VICTORY IN WARFARE

We are taking every thought captive to the obedience of Christ.

—2 Corinthians 10:5

CHAPTER NINE

THE TRANSFORMED HEART

The Lord has not promised us a world without hardship, but that in the midst of hardship He will be revealed through us.

CHRIST: THE GREAT I AM

What is God's primary purpose for us? Why were we created? From the beginning of time, God created man with one purpose: to make us in His image, according to His likeness.

The Lord has never changed His divine intent toward us. Indeed, Paul tells us that God causes all things in our lives to work toward the good of this one eternal goal (Rom. 8:28–29). What of the difficulties and tribulations that we encounter in this life? In the scheme of God's plan, troubles and afflictions are upgraded to classroom lessons where we learn to appropriate the nature of Christ. Our difficulties compel us toward God, and He compels us toward Christlikeness and change.

Thus, the Lord speaks to each of us His promise,

"Do not fear, for I have redeemed you; I have called you by name; you are Mine! When you pass through the waters, I will be with you; and through the rivers, they will not overflow you. When you walk through the fire, you will not be scorched, nor will the flame burn you. For I am the Lord your God, the Holy One of Israel, your Savior."   —Isaiah 43:1–3

While His pledge is a great encouragement, we should be mindful that the Lord did not say He would keep us from the fire or the floodwaters, but He would be with us in them. Why does the Lord allow us to pass through conflict in the first place? Because it is here that He trains His sons and daughters in Christlikeness.

Recall the story of Jesus' disciples when they were without Him on a turbulent sea (Matt. 14:22–33). Their boat had been battered by the heaving waves and contrary wind. Jesus, walking on the water, came to them sometime in the early morning. His first words were those of comfort. He said, "Take courage, it is I; do not be afraid" (Matt. 14:27).

THE FATHER'S HIGHEST PURPOSE

It is important to note that the words Christ uses in His assurance, "It is I," is translated other places within Scripture as, "I Am." This phrase is the divine appellation – the eternal designation of God. While Jesus indeed comes to the aid of His disciples, He also reveals Himself transcendent of time's barriers. As such, He proclaims His availability to *all* His disciples. He is God with us, even to the end of the age!

Thus, Jesus still comes to His disciples' aid, manifesting Himself in the storms of our times, defying what seem to be impossible conditions in order to reach us. He is the master of every human distress; He can help us in every circumstance.

Let us silence the fretting unbelief of our hearts. *Christ is capable, even at this moment, to reach us.* Look through the storm until you sense

His presence – until you hear His confident voice saying, *"Take courage, it is I."*

Yet Jesus has more on His mind than comforting His disciples. It is one thing to trust Christ to calm the storm around us; it is another matter to leave our security and venture out with Him on the water! This very setting of raging wind and sea is the classroom in which the Son of God seeks to perfect His disciples' faith.

Let us affirm the Father's highest purpose for us: Jesus did not come simply to console us but to perfect us! This is exactly where He will take us once we are willing. To behold Christ's goal for us of perfection is to truly gaze into another dimension of God.

We should repent of carrying the image of a Savior who fails to confront our sin or challenge our unbelief, for such is a false image of God. If we are to genuinely know Him, we must accept this truth: *Jesus Christ is irrevocably committed to our complete transformation!*

Compelled Toward God

Of all the disciples, Peter alone responds to the occasion with vision and faith. Putting his hands on the upper plank of the rolling boat's side, Peter peers through the dark night and windblown spray. He calls to Jesus, "Lord, if it is You, command me to come to You on the water" (Matt. 14:28). There is faith in Peter's voice!

Jesus summons His disciple: "Come!"

Peter swings his legs over the edge, dangling them above the swirling sea. With his eyes fixed on Jesus, he steps out, letting his full weight follow both the downward movement of his feet and the upward reach of his faith. Incredibly, Peter is now standing and walking on the rolling waves toward Jesus!

In the purest sense, however, Peter did not rest his weight on the water; he stood upon Christ's word: *"Come!"* Peter trusted that if Jesus told him to do the impossible – even to walk on the water – the power to obey would be inherent within the command.

We know that moments later Peter's faith faltered. He began to sink. But there is something extraordinary to be seen in Christ's response – a view into Christ's actual nature and His ultimate purpose. Jesus did not commend or congratulate Peter. He *rebuked* him! We would have expected praise and encouragement, but none came.

Was Jesus angry? No. The truth is, Jesus Christ is relentlessly given to our perfection. He knows that wherever we settle spiritually will be far short of His provision. He also knows that the more we are transformed into His image, the less vulnerable we are to the evils of this world. Thus He compels us toward difficulties, for they compel us toward God, and God compels us toward change. And it is the transformed heart that finds the shelter of the Most High.

Let's pray: *Lord Jesus, forgive me for fearing during the storms of life. For too long I have not understood Your commitment to my perfection. I have wanted to be saved without being transformed. I have feared the fullness of becoming Christlike. Bring forth in me Your faith; help me to not misinterpret Your encouragement toward excellence when I fall short. With all my heart, I want to glorify You with my life. Grant me the grace that, when others see what You have accomplished in me, they, too, shall glorify You! Amen.*

—FROM THE BOOK *THE SHELTER OF THE MOST HIGH*

SELF TEST, CHAPTER NINE

Remember, we are looking for answers that correspond with this training. Please write out your answers, allowing the Holy Spirit to provoke your thoughts. You may want to use them for group discussion. Note: we do not provide answers to questions you write out. To check your multiple choice answers, see answer key in the next session.

Chapter 9, Question #1: List the values of possessing a transformed heart.

1. The Lord has not promised us a world without hardship, but that in the midst of hardship He will be:
   a. absent
   b. in hardship also
   c. revealed through us
   d. hiding

2. Our difficulties:
   a. compel us toward Christlikeness
   b. compel us toward God
   c. compel us toward change
   d. all the above

3. The Lord allows us to pass through conflict:
   a. to train us
   b. to see how long we can fake being nice
   c. to prove we need help
   d. for no reason

4. Jesus still comes to His disciples' aid today, manifesting Himself during storms:
   a. but only during movies
   b. to scare us
   c. so we can see Him
   d. to prove He can reach us no matter what our circumstances

5. It is one thing to trust Christ to calm the storm around us; it is another matter to:
   a. call the weather channel and wait for a clear day
   b. leave our security and venture out with Him on the water
   c. stay in the boat and criticize others
   d. sleep during the storm

6. Jesus Christ is irrevocably committed to:
   a. our complete transformation
   b. limiting our spiritual maturity
   c. turning water into grape drinks
   d. using mud to cure blindness

7. Jesus knows that the more we are transformed into His image:
   a. the more we will know
   b. the more prideful we will become
   c. the less vulnerable we are to the evils of this world
   d. the less we'll have to go to church

8. Jesus, with all my heart I want to glorify You with:
   a. gold
   b. incense
   c. my life
   d. myrrh

CHAPTER TEN

THE STRONGHOLD
OF CHRISTLIKENESS

Victory begins with the name of Jesus on our lips.
It is consummated by the nature of Jesus in our hearts.

GOD'S HIGHEST PURPOSE

Most Christians only seek God with a hope of either relieving present distresses or attaining a comparatively "normal" existence. However, the purpose of all aspects of spirituality is to bring us into the image of Christ. Nothing spiritual can be fully realized – not worship, warfare, love or deliverance – if we miss the singular objective of our faith: Christ's likeness.

Let us recall that the Lord delivered the ancient Hebrews out of Egypt so He could bring them into the Promised Land. Likewise, we are delivered out of sin not that we might live for ourselves but that we might possess the likeness of Christ. Indeed, the promised land for a Christian is to manifest the fullness of Christ. Thus, our goals must align with God's. For if our nature does not change, we will invariably find ourselves entangled in the same problems that caused our difficulties in the first place.

While we may not want to hear this, many of our spiritual conflicts simply are not going to cease until the character of the Lord Jesus is formed in our hearts. The Father's goal in deliverance is much more than simply relieving our burdens or having the devil taken off our backs.

Indeed, God is working all things in our lives toward one specific purpose, which is to conform us "to the image of His Son." The Father's purpose in our salvation was that Jesus would become "the firstborn among many brethren." In other words, the way to realize God's ultimate victory is to reach toward His ultimate goal, which is our transformation into the likeness of Christ.

When we come to Christ, an interpenetration of spirits occurs between God and ourselves. In this place of union there exists a divine potential for the surrendered, believing Christian: *Our spirits are fully saturated with the living presence of the Lord Jesus.*

This inner abiding place is the God-created life source where we, "with unveiled face," can behold "the glory of the Lord." It is in this secret place with God where we are "transformed into [Christ's] image from glory to glory" (2 Cor. 3:18). In this place the glory of God can so flood our inner life that there is "no dark part" left within us (Luke 11:36).

This immediacy of the Lord's presence produces an indestructible defense, a fortress within, where we can be hidden from evil. As we enter the excellence of His ways, we ascend into a place of spiritual immunity where we can be hidden from countless satanic attacks. Indeed, as His fullness within us increases, that which is written is fulfilled: "As He is, so also are we in this world" and "He who was born of God keeps [us], and the evil one does not touch [us]" (1 John 4:17; 5:18).

We must realize that it is not Satan who defeats us as much as it is our openness to him. Therefore, to perfectly subdue the devil God must subdue us;

our anxious, selfish thoughts must be arrested until we dwell in peace within the "shelter of the Most High" (Ps. 91:1). Satan is tolerated for one purpose: The warfare between the devil and God's saints thrusts us into Christlikeness where the nature of Christ becomes our only place of rest and security.

Once we realize that the Father's goal is to transform our lives, we will continually find that God has one answer to spiritual conflicts: *Appropriate the nature of His Son!*

Are you troubled by a spirit of fear or doubt? Submit those areas to God, repenting of your unbelief, and then yield yourself to the gift of faith that exists within you through the Holy Spirit. Are you troubled with spirits of lust and shame? Present those very areas of sin to God, repenting of your old nature, and draw upon the forgiveness of Christ and His purity of heart.

The Father is more concerned with the coming forth of His Son in our lives than He is in defeating Satan. Who is the devil that he can defy the living God? Indeed, it is of the greatest truth in discerning the attack of the enemy that once he recognizes his assault against you has not pulled you from God but driven you toward Him – once he perceives that his temptations are actually forcing you to appropriate the virtue of Christ – the enemy will withdraw.

The Goal Is Christlikeness, Not Warfare

There is a time when the Lord will call us to confront the strongholds of hell over our churches and our communities. There is another time, however, when to engage in much spiritual warfare is actually a distraction from your obedience to God. Jesus defeated Satan in Gethsemane and at the cross, not by directly confronting the devil but by fulfilling the destiny to which He had been called at Calvary. *The greatest battle that was ever won was accomplished by the apparent death of the victor, without even a word of rebuke to His adversary!* The prince of this world was judged and principalities and powers were disarmed not by confrontational warfare but by the surrender of Jesus Christ on the cross.

There are occasions when your battle against the devil is actually a digression from the higher purpose God has for you. Intercessors and warfare leaders take note: There is a demon whose purpose is to lure one's mind into hell. If we were to name this spirit, we would call it "Wrong Focus." You may be fighting this very spirit if you are continually seeing evil spirits in people or in the material world around you. The ultimate goal of this demon is to produce mental illness in saints who move in deliverance. Listen very carefully: We are not called to focus on the battle or the devil, except when that battle hinders our immediate transformation into Christ's likeness. Our calling is to focus on Jesus. The work of the devil, however, is to draw our eyes from Jesus. Satan's first weapon always involves luring our eyes from Christ. Turn toward Jesus and almost immediately the battle vanishes.

I knew a man once who owned a record company. Besides running the operation, he also spent many hours in production listening to the "mother disk," which was the master from which all subsequent recordings were produced. Over the years, his ears became adept at catching the "pops and sizzles," the imperfections that had to be eliminated in the master. I remarked one day that I thought working with music must be enjoyable. His response was enlightening. He said, "You know, I haven't listened to music in years. When I turn on my sophisticated home stereo, no matter what recording I'm listening to, all I hear are the pops and sizzles."

In the same way his thoughts were bent toward musical imperfections, so Wrong Focus will seek to turn your thoughts continually toward the enemy. Suddenly, all you will see are demons. The true gift called "discerning of spirits" is a balanced gift which enables you to recognize at least as many angelic spirits as you do evil spirits. The proper manifestation of this gift has a much more positive focus and influence than what commonly masquerades as discernment.

An example of the proper balance in discernment is seen in 2 Kings. The Syrian army had surrounded Dothan, a city in Israel, much to the consternation of the prophet Elisha's servant. To calm his attendant's fright, Elisha prayed that his servant's eyes would be opened. He then encouraged his servant, saying, "Do not fear, for those who are with us are more than those who are with them" (2 Kings 6:16). As the Lord opened the servant's eyes, he saw what Elisha saw: "The mountain was full of horses and chariots of fire all around Elisha" (v. 17).

In spiritual warfare, the battle is never limited to an "us against them" human affair. It always includes "those … with us" against "those … with them." True discernment is as fully aware of the vast multitude of angels loyal to God as it is aware of the activity of the demonic realm – and it is aware that the angelic hosts on our side are both stronger and more numerous than the enemy. Remember, if you fail to "hear the music" in your times of warfare, your discernment is incomplete.

We must learn that, on a personal level, it is better to develop godly virtues than to spend our day praying against the devil. Indeed, it is the joy of the Lord that casts out spirits of depression. It is our living faith which destroys spirits of unbelief; it is aggressive love which casts out fear.

As we continually yield ourselves to Christ, surrendering ourselves by faith to His nature and His words, we literally build the impenetrable strong-hold of His presence around us. The way into the fortress of the Almighty is simple. Victory begins with the name of Jesus on our lips. It is consum-mated by the nature of Jesus in our hearts.

Let's pray: *Lord Jesus, help me to keep my eyes fixed on You. You are my strong tower and my fortress. Show me areas in my soul that are easily manipulated by the enemy. Reveal to me where I am harboring darkness, that I might dwell in the impenetrable shelter of Your light!*

—FROM THE BOOK *THE THREE BATTLEGROUNDS*

SELF TEST, CHAPTER TEN

Remember, we are looking for answers that correspond with this train-ing. Please write out your answers, allowing the Holy Spirit to provoke your thoughts. You may want to use them for group discussion. Note: we do not provide answers to questions you write out. To check your multiple choice answers, see answer key in the next session.

Chapter 10, Question #1: Explain this statement: It is not Satan who defeats us; it is our *openness* to him.

1. Nothing spiritual can be fully realized – not worship, warfare, love or deliverance – if we miss the singular objective of our faith: _____.
    a. mercy
    b. Christ's likeness
    c. justice
    d. miracles

2. Many of our spiritual conflicts simply are not going to cease until:
    a. the character of the Lord Jesus is formed in our hearts
    b. we get our warfare just right
    c. we have our marching orders
    d. we pray more and more

3. The immediacy of the Lord's presence produces:
    a. an indestructible defense
    b. a fortress within
    c. goose bumps
    d. both a & b

4. God has one answer to spiritual conflicts:
    a. which is always painful
    b. appropriate the nature of His Son
    c. the proper techniques must be learned to combat
       conflicts
    d. call your mother

5. There can be times when to engage in much spiritual
  warfare is actually:
    a. exhausting
    b. sinful
    c. a distraction from your obedience to God
    d. very time consuming

6. We are not called to focus on the battle or the devil,
  except when that battle:
    a. involves us
    b. appears huge
    c. rages
    d. hinders our immediate transformation into
       Christ's likeness

7. "Discerning of spirits" is a balanced gift which enables
  us to recognize at least as many _____ as _____
  spirits:
    a. loud, quiet
    b. large, small
    c. angelic, evil
    d. short, tall

8. Do not fear, for those who are with us are _____
  than those who are with them (2 Kings 6:16).
    a. more
    b. fewer
    c. stronger
    d. both a & c

> QUOTE:
>
> *"Victory begins with the name of Jesus on our lips. It is consummated by the nature of Jesus in our hearts."*

SESSION SIX:

THE TRIUMPH OF CHRIST'S LIFE

And we know that God causes all things to work together for good to those who love God, to those who are called according to His purpose. For those whom He foreknew, He also predestined to become conformed to the image of His Son, so that He would be the firstborn among many brethren. —Romans 8:28–29

SESSION SIX AUDIO MESSAGES:

6a. The Foundation of Christlikeness
6b. Unoffendable

Lessons are to be distributed from
the Training Center only, please.

ANSWER KEY TO LAST SESSION'S
SELF TEST QUESTIONS:

CHAPTER NINE. The Transformed Heart
1.c, 2.d, 3.a, 4.d, 5.b, 6.a, 7.c, 8.c.

CHAPTER TEN. The Stronghold of Christlikeness
1.b, 2.a, 3.d, 4.b, 5.c, 6.d, 7.c, 8.d.

CHAPTER ELEVEN

TRUE SUCCESS

> That I may know Him, and the power of His resurrection and the fellowship of His sufferings, being conformed to His death; in order that I may attain to the resurrection from the dead.
> —Philippians 3:10–11

This training series is about one thing: the church becoming Christlike. Unity is the consequence of Christlikeness; power is the result of Christlikeness; conversions are because of our Christlikeness; healed families, miracles and eternal life – all spring from one central source: becoming like Jesus in everything. If our goal is something other than conformity to Christ, besides being spiritually unfulfilled, we will inevitably be left vulnerable to deception, sin and divisions.

When I speak of becoming Christlike, I mean a few specific love-motivated realities, such as humility, submissiveness, intercessory prayer, and a mature, redemptive attitude of heart.

TRUE HUMILITY

Beloved, all of us need to seek God for a true revelation of Christ's humility. Jesus said the humble are "the greatest" in His kingdom (Matt. 18:4). In the church today, among leaders and congregations alike, we need the humility Jesus demonstrated when He girded Himself and washed His disciples' feet (John 13:4–5). This is not an imposed humility but a choice we make as we seek the nature of the Savior.

Paul tells us to have in us the same attitude that we see in Christ who, existing in the form of God, did not regard His equality with the Father as a thing to be grasped but emptied Himself of His privileges and, in humility, took the form of a man – and then died for men! (Phil. 2:5–8). In other words, Jesus saw the need – as terrible as it was – and came to redeem it. He could have simply destroyed the earth; He could have ignored our need. Instead He died for us. His footsteps are the will of God for me. With all my heart I desire to walk as He did: without fear, motivated by love, empowered to make a difference, and willing to die for those who would crucify me.

Submissiveness

When I speak of becoming Christlike, it includes being submissive to authority. Jesus grew up in subjection to His parents; He insisted on submitting Himself to John's baptism, though He was clearly John's spiritual superior. He submitted Himself to the injustice of Pilate's secular authority, while entrusting Himself without fear to the power of the Father who judges righteously. Christ's eyes were not on Pilate but upon the Father who, in His omnipotence, would soon take every injustice and make it part of the plan of redemption. So, Jesus could submit to man because He had faith in God, the Father.

When we make our goal the meekness and submissiveness of Christ, we know we can trust God with our future. Then we have no problem serving the vision and ministry of someone else along the way. And ambition, a cause of so many church splits, has no power among us.

PRAYER AND A REDEMPTIVE HEART ATTITUDE

To seek Christlikeness means that when I see something wrong in the born-again church, or even in the world, I am capable of looking at it maturely without panic. Because I am a person of prayer, I trust that God has a redemptive answer. Do you recall how Jesus handled the demon-possessed man in Gerasenes? The individual confronted Jesus as He passed among the tombs; broken chains dragged from his wrists and ankles. Yet within minutes Jesus had restored the man to his right mind, delivering him of the tormenting demons that possessed him (Mark 5:1–15). The same Jesus who calmed the demoniac dwells in us. He doesn't want us to be swallowed up by what is wrong; He calls us to transform it.

My call to you, beloved, is to walk as Christ walked, in humility and submission, so we can present to Him a church without spot or blemish or any such thing (Eph. 5:27). Let us persevere in trials, knowing God sees and judges. Let us define success, not merely as having a name known on earth, but attaining Christlikeness and possessing a name known and honored in Heaven.

Let's pray: *Lord Jesus, I see in You all I want to be. I desire with all my heart to be like You, Lord. You have promised that a pupil shall become like his master. Fulfill Your promise in me! Transform me, so the world will see and worship You. Help me to define true success as attaining one goal: possessing Your glorious nature. Amen.*

—FROM THE BOOK *A HOUSE UNITED*

SELF TEST, CHAPTER ELEVEN

Remember, we are looking for answers that correspond with this training. Please write out your answers, allowing the Holy Spirit to provoke your thoughts. You may want to use them for group discussion. Note: we do not provide answers to questions you write out. To check your multiple choice answers, see answer key in the next session.

Chapter 11, Question #1: Describe true success.

1. The results of Christlikeness are:
   a. healed families
   b. power and miracles
   c. unity and eternal life
   d. all the above

2. Jesus said the _____ were the greatest in His kingdom (Matt. 18:4).
   a. wealthiest
   b. kings
   c. disciples
   d. humble

3. When we make our goal the meekness and submissiveness of Christ, we know we can:
   a. expect to be persecuted
   b. trust God with our future
   c. choose our destiny
   d. feel secure

4. God calls us:
   a. to transform what is wrong
   b. to sing in the choir
   c. because the line was busy in Jerusalem
   d. because He needs an answer

5. Christlikeness includes:
   a. rebellion
   b. murmuring
   c. hiding things under tents
   d. being submissive to authority

6. Success is not merely having a name known on earth, but attaining:
   a. a pulpit
   b. Christlikeness
   c. a great name
   d. financial gain

QUOTE:

"This training series is about one thing: the church becoming Christlike. Unity is the consequence of Christlikeness; power is the result of Christlikeness; conversions are because of our Christlikeness; healed families, miracles and eternal life – all spring from one central source: becoming like Jesus in everything!

CHAPTER TWELVE

UNOFFENDABLE

"I will give you a new heart and put a new spirit within you; and I will remove the heart of stone from your flesh and give you a heart of flesh."   —Ezekiel 36:26

God has a new heart for us that cannot be offended – an "unoffendable" heart. Beloved, possessing an unoffendable heart is not an option or a luxury; it's not a little thing. An offended heart is in danger of becoming a "heart of stone." Jesus warns that as we near the end of the age a majority of people will be offended to such a degree that they fall away from the faith. Listen carefully to His warning:

Then shall many be offended, and shall betray one another, and shall hate one another ... and because iniquity shall abound, the love of many shall wax cold.
            —Matthew 24:10–12 KJV

"Many" will be offended. The result? The love of "many" will grow cold. My prayer is that we will hear His words with holy fear.

THE DANGER OF HARBORING OFFENSE

When we allow an offense to ferment in our hearts, it causes serious spiritual consequences. In the above verse Jesus named three dangerous results: betrayal, hatred and cold love. When we are offended with someone, even someone we care for, we must go to them. *If we do not talk to them, we will begin to talk about them.* We betray that relationship, whispering maliciously behind their back to others, exposing their weaknesses and sins.

We may mask our betrayal by saying we are just looking for advice or counsel, but when we look back, we see we have spoken negatively about that person to far too many people. Our real goal was not to get spiritual help for ourselves but to seek revenge toward the one who offended us. How is such action not a manifestation of hatred? For an offended soul, cold love, betrayal and hatred are a walk into darkness.

People don't stumble over boulders; they stumble over stones, relatively small things. It may be that the personality of someone in authority bothers us, and soon we are offended. Or a friend or family member fails to meet our expectations, and we take an offense into our soul. Beloved, if we will "endure to the end" (Matt. 24:13), we will have to confront the things that bother us.

When Jesus warns that we need endurance, He is saying that it is easier to begin the race than finish it. Between now and the day you die, you will face major times of offense that you will need to overcome. You might be in such a time right now. Do not minimize the danger of harboring an offense.

No one plans on falling away; no one ever says, "Today I think I'll try to develop a hardened heart of stone." Such things enter our souls through stealth. It is only naiveté that assumes it couldn't happen to us. I know many people who consistently become offended about one thing or another. Instead of dealing with the offenses, praying about them and turning the issue over to God, they carry the offense in their soul until its weight disables their walk with God. You may be doing fine today, but I guarantee you that tomorrow something will happen that will inevitably disappoint or wound you; some injustice will strike you, demanding you retaliate in the flesh. Will you find more love and, hence, continue your growth toward Christlikeness? Or will you allow that offense to consume your spiritual life?

THE ROOT OF OFFENSE

An offense can strike at our virtues or sins, our values or our pride. It can penetrate and wound any dimension of the soul, both good and evil. I once brought a series of messages about gossip. Most people saw their sin and repented, but a core group of gossips was greatly offended and ultimately left the church. When the Holy Spirit exposes sin in someone's soul, if we refuse the opportunity to repent, we often become offended at the person who brought the teaching. Instead of humbling our hearts, we are outraged at the person who exposed us. Truthfully, most of the time, I have no idea who specifically needs to hear what I'm teaching, but God knows.

Paul told Timothy to "reprove, rebuke, exhort" (2 Tim. 4:2). He didn't say, "exhort, exhort, exhort," but exhortation is what we receive in most churches. People do not change by exhortation alone. Certainly we need to be encouraged, but there are also times, beloved, when we need to be reproved and rebuked. There are areas in all of us that need to be confronted and disciplined.

Today there are preachers who are afraid to preach truth for fear people will react and leave the church. The end result is a church of easily offended people who cannot grow beyond their inability to accept correction. The leader who refuses to discipline and correct those in sin is in disobedience to God. He is unable to lead people into any truly transforming changes in their lives;

they will not obtain Christlikeness if they cannot be corrected.

We need to become a people who say, "Lord, show me what needs to change in me." I'm talking about growing up. A wise man will receive a rebuke and will prosper, but "a fool rejects his father's discipline" (Prov. 15:5).

Personal Offense

It is often our pride that suffers offense most easily. Pride leads us to expect more than we deserve. Pride is a form of self-worship. God must destroy our pride, and to do so He will allow offenses to expose what we lack in humility. It is not wrong to expect encouragement for our good works, but we cannot be offended when it doesn't happen in the timing we are expecting.

Years ago when I was a young pastor, my wife and I attended a conference where the main leader decided to personally greet each minister and spouse. He greeted the couple on our right and then turned to his staff to ask a question. A moment later he returned but passed us by and went to the couple on our left. Everyone around us saw we were bypassed. We were embarrassed and offended. But my wife wisely observed that we could allow this thing to hurt us or we could see it as an investment in sensitivity toward other people's feelings. The offense taught us how others feel when they are ignored. Do you see this? You must make that offense become an opportunity to become more Christlike.

The occasions for taking offense are practically endless. Indeed, we are daily given the opportunity to either be offended by something or to possess an unoffendable heart. The Lord's promise is that He's given us a new heart – a soft, entreatable heart that can be filled with His Spirit and abound with His love.

Through the years, I have learned some things about the nature of Christ and how He handles the offenses of this world. Most of these I am still working on, but to a real degree they are living realities in my heart.

One thing I've learned is to humble myself when I'm criticized; instead of reacting or defending myself, I try to listen and consider what I'm being told. I've been wrong enough times in life to know that perhaps the person speaking to me is right. They actually may see something about me in an area where I've been blind. Of course, being confronted by someone is never joyful. Indeed, when an individual finally has enough nerve to openly speak about what bothers them, their approach, which should be in gentleness, may come across as nervous and unnecessarily confrontational.

Yet if they are even partially right in their opinion, we can make good use of their complaint. Humility listens even to a harshly spoken word and without reacting rescues the truth within the criticism. The result is that we discover an area we had not seen, and instead of being offended we become more Christlike.

It might be that a criticism is not true and a person's opinion about us seems almost insulting. However, their words can still be helpful in that they may spotlight a weakness in how we present ourselves to others. We could have right motives, but be less than perfect in our communication. Here, too, we gain insight and make progress from another's criticism. We can always improve our approach so that we are more sensitive to how others perceive us.

If an attack is not based on truth, and the person is simply a source of persecution and slander, how can we grow in that circumstance? Recall, Jesus tells us to "pray for those who persecute you" (Matt. 5:44) and "bless those who curse you" (Luke 6:28). Thus, instead of being offended by something that was obviously vicious, we grow in the love and intercession of Christ who, as He died, prayed, "Father, forgive them."

Remember, Jesus said offenses were inevitable. He warned that we were going to have frequent, almost daily, opportunities to be offended by the injustices of life. When life cuts us, do we bleed anger and revenge, or do we look to God and appropriate the heart of Christ? There will always be attacks from misguided, even demonically possessed, people. The issue isn't whether or not we are wounded, but what we do when we are hurt. When we fail to process the wounding as Christ would, anger floods our souls, and the wound degrades into bitterness. Clinically, we are offended, and a form of spiritual paralysis immobilizes our walk with God.

I want to clarify that there are some things in life that demand our outrage. Brutal killings, child abuse or blatant sin in the world around us should create an appropriate disturbance in our spirits. Ultimately, though, our reaction must be vented to God in prayer. The outrage must spur either intercession or action on our part to stop the injustice; even in this process we must guard our hearts. What does it profit us if we gain the victory but lose our capacity to love?

Remember always, God is causing all things to work together for good in your life. If you know His goal in everything is to create the likeness of Christ in you, then no weapon formed against you will prosper. You will possess the unoffendable heart of Christ.

Let's pray: *Lord, forgive me for being so easily offended and for carrying offenses. Father, my heart is often foolish, weak and defensive. Yet I trust in*

Your promise that I am a new creation. With faith I ask, grant me the unoffendable heart of Jesus Christ. Amen.

—ADAPTED FROM THE BOOK *A HOUSE UNITED*

SELF TEST, CHAPTER TWELVE

Remember, we are looking for answers that correspond with this training. Please write out your answers, allowing the Holy Spirit to provoke your thoughts. You may want to use them for group discussion. Note: we do not provide answers to questions you write out. To check your multiple choice answers, see answer key at the end of this session.

Chapter 12, Question #1: Why is it so much easier to start the race than to finish it?

1. God has a new heart for us – an _____ heart:
   a. inflexible
   b. unyielding
   c. unoffendable
   d. unbreakable

2. When we allow an offense to ferment in our hearts, it can cause:
   a. cold love
   b. betrayal
   c. hatred
   d. all the above

3. People don't stumble over _____; they stumble over _____.
   a. trees, logs
   b. boulders, stones
   c. steps, small cracks
   d. truth, lies

4. When it comes to running the race set before us, it is easier to begin the race than to:
   a. run at all
   b. finish it
   c. stop it
   d. change lanes

5. The apostle Paul didn't say "exhort, exhort, exhort." He said, exhort,
   a. reprove
   b. approach
   c. rebuke
   d. both a & c

6. There are areas in our lives that need to be:
   a. meddled in
   b. confronted
   c. disciplined
   d. both b & c

7. We must make offenses become:
   a. wounds
   b. null & void
   c. opportunities to grow in Christ
   d. routine

8. Lord, grant me an:
   a. unbreakable heart
   b. unoffendable heart
   c. touchable heart
   d. unloveable heart

Lessons are to be distributed from the Training Center only, please.

ANSWER KEY TO THIS SESSION'S SELF TEST QUESTIONS:

CHAPTER ELEVEN. True Success
1.d, 2.d, 3.b, 4.a, 5.d, 6.b.

CHAPTER TWELVE. Unoffendable
1.c, 2.d, 3.b, 4.b, 5.d, 6.d, 7.c, 8.b.

Online Resources for

In Christ's Image Training

Online School Information

ICIT online school was established to empower individuals seeking greater conformity to Christ. Students from around the world register online and then receive two written messages each week via email. They also receive a set of 39 audio teachings (on 24 CDs or MP3s), which complement the written messages and add to the training. Students are then tested every six weeks and receive a cumulative grade at the end of six months; they also receive Level I certification from *In Christ's Image Training*.

The text materials used by our online school have been upgraded and reproduced into these four Level I manuals. If you are interested in continuing your studies, or if you desire certification through *In Christ's Image Training,* you will need to purchase and study the audio messages that accompany these manuals (see the following resource pages). You will then need to take a separate exam that will confirm to us that you have understood the training materials and are, indeed, pursuing the character of Christ.

For more information about current prices, special offers and the benefits of *In Christ's Image Training,* visit our web site at www.ICITC.org. No one will be refused training due to lack of funds. We have several options to consider for those who are unable to submit full tuition for Level I. We are available to discuss these options with you. Email us at training@inchristsimage.org.

In Christ's Image Training is now available in Spanish. Please contact us at spanish@inchristsimage.org for more information.

Curriculum Package Options

Level I Premium Package
(Enrollment in *ICIT* Online School)

When enrolled in ICIT Level I Online School, the commitment is for six months of training via weekly email lessons. Testing will be done every six weeks, following the completion of each track (Christlikeness, Humility, Prayer, Unity).

Individual Tuition	$250
Married Couple	$350
Group Rate (per person, in group of four or more)	$90

See our website for any special online prices. Training also available in Spanish.

Materials provided:
>Sessions introduced through weekly email
>39 audio messages on 24 CDs or MP3 downloads (included in tuition)

Benefits of Enrollment in *ICIT* Level I Online School:
>Comprehensive final exam
>Grading and administration at our Training Center
>Graduation certificate from ICIT/Pastor Frangipane
>Invitation to our 3-day seminars
>Invitation to join our Global Student Directory
>Opportunity to continue to Level II: Growing in Christ
>Opportunity to continue to Level III: Facilitation
>Opportunity to join Advancing Church Ministries Association
>Special offers on books and Pastor Frangipane's CD albums
>Opportunity to purchase seminar media at discounted prices

For more information visit www.ICITC.org.

*NOTE: As an ICIT Level I online student, you are entitled to purchase one set of study manuals from Arrow Publications at 50% of the retail price.

Level I Basic Training
(using Arrow Publications materials)
In Basic Training, the student/group studies at their own pace.

Full course: manuals and audio messages	retail $168	our price $164
Manuals only (4 books: Christlikeness, Humility, Prayer, Unity)	retail $48	our price $44
Audio only (24 CDs or MP3s)		$120

Materials available: Four manuals and 39 audio messages
>(see back of Unity book for session and audio title listing)

*Note: If you purchased this Basic Training package, you can still later enroll in the online school. To officially complete Level I and receive ICIT certification, you must enroll in our online school and successfully pass the final exam, after studying all manuals and audio teachings. Tuition cost for completion of Level I is $72. Visit www.ICITC.org for Level II tuition fees.

ICIT Member Churches/Organizations

ICIT member churches/organizations may receive substantial discounts or other benefits for your church or organization when you purchase ICIT materials through Arrow Publications. For the most current offers and news, visit www.ICITC.org.

FRANCIS FRANGIPANE

BOOKS BY THEME

RELATIONSHIP WITH CHRIST

HOLINESS, TRUTH AND THE PRESENCE OF GOD. A penetrating study of the human heart and how God prepares it for His glory. *Published by Charisma House.*

THE SHELTER OF THE MOST HIGH. Francis gives trustworthy, biblical evidence that in the midst of all our uncertainties and fears there is an available shelter from God to shield us. Once you have found this place, nothing you encounter can defeat you. This is a revised and expanded version of *The Stronghold of God. Published by Charisma House.*

THE POWER OF ONE CHRISTLIKE LIFE. The prayer of a Christlike intercessor is the most powerful force in the universe, delaying God's wrath until He pours out His mercy.

I WILL BE FOUND BY YOU. The essence of *I Will Be Found by You* is a living promise from God. If we genuinely, from our heart, pursue the Lord, He promises He will meet us. Francis calls the church to a focused season of seeking God. We must have more of God, and if it is God we desire, it is God we shall find! *Published by Passio (div of Charisma House Book Group).*

UNITY

A HOUSE UNITED. Few works of the enemy are as destructive to the body of Christ as a church split. Once a wedge is driven into the heart of a congregation, the result is usually bitterness, grief, even hatred among those who are called to live together in love. This is an expanded version of the book *It's Time to End Church Splits. Published by Chosen Books.*

WHEN THE MANY ARE ONE. How the Christian community – driven by grace, unified in love, and activated by prayer – can bring revival and change. This is a revised and expanded version of *The House of the Lord. Published by Charisma House.*

Francis Frangipane
BOOKS BY THEME

Prophetic

The Days of His Presence. As the day of the Lord draws near, though darkness covers the earth, the outraying of Christ's presence shall arise and appear upon His people! *Published by Charisma House.*

Spiritual Warfare

The Three Battlegrounds. *Revised Edition:* An in-depth view of three arenas of spiritual warfare: the mind, the church and the heavenly places.

The Power of Covenant Prayer. Gain the victory over the effect of curses. The section on persevering prayer is a must for anyone serious about attaining Christlikeness. The second part is the conclusion of a teaching on spiritual protection. Powerful insights on the nature of curses and how to walk in spiritual victory and freedom. (Formerly titled *The Divine Antidote*). *Published by Charisma House.*

This Day We Fight. We cannot be passive and also win the war for our souls. Pastor Frangipane exposes the disarming that occurs when we accept a passive spirit into our thoughts. The passive spirit seems innocent, yet it causes us to stop seeking God, ultimately rendering us defenseless against spiritual attack and the weaknesses of our flesh. This is essential reading for the overcoming church. *Published by Chosen Books.*

Spiritual Discernment and the Mind of Christ. In a world where hearts harden quickly with every new outrage that emerges in society – where the love of many is growing cold, Pastor Francis unveils the glory of possessing the mind of Christ. This book will open the door not only to sense the Lord's presence but to actually hear His heart and gain discernment from His perspective.

TO ORDER MINISTRY RESOURCES: www.arrowbookstore.com
FOR TEACHINGS/CONFERENCES: www.frangipane.org